Winged

Words

Winged

Words

American Indian Writers Speak

Laura Coltelli

University of Nebraska Press

Lincoln and London

Manufactured in the United States of America
First Bison Book printing: 1992
Most recent printing indicated by the
last digit below:
10 9 8 7 6 5 4 3 2 1
Library of Congress Cataloging in Publication Data
Coltelli, Laura, 1941 –
Winged words : American Indian writers speak /
Laura Coltelli.
p.   cm. – (American Indian lives) Includes
bibliographical references.
Contents: Introduction – Paula Gunn Allen –
Louise Erdrich and
Michael Dorris – Joy Harjo – Linda Hogan –
N. Scott Momaday –
Simon Ortiz – Wendy Rose – Leslie Marmon Silko –
Gerald Vizenor –
James Welch. ISBN 0-8032-1445-6 (alk. paper)
ISBN 0-8032-6351-1 (pbk.)
1. American literature –
Indian authors – History and criticism.
2. American literature –
20th century – History and criticism.
3. Authors, American –
20th century – Interviews. 4. Indians of North
America – Interviews.
5. Authors, Indian – Interviews. 6. Indians in literature.
I. Title. II. Series.
PS153.152C57   1990 810.9′897 – dc20
89-39323   CIP

♾

To the memory
of my father,
Vittorio Coltelli,
1903–1987,
faithful friend to
many Indians.

Indian Country, 1972.
Remembering a vintage year.

Contents

Acknowledgments

I would like to express my appreciation to the Council for International Exchange of Scholars, which partially supported my project with a Fulbright Fellowship. I wish also to thank Kenneth Lincoln for his advice and guidance and for providing me with invaluable resources and information. I owe a special debt of gratitude to the UCLA American Indian Studies Center and the Institute of American Cultures for a postdoctoral fellowship to carry on my project. I am also grateful to all the staff of the UCLA American Indian Studies Center and to the librarian, Velma S. Salabiye, for their help and assistance.

Very special thanks to M. L. Rosenthal and to Kathleen Mullen Sands, A. LaVonne Brown Ruoff, and Larry Evers for their support and encouragement. I wish also to express my thanks to Cinzia Biagiotti for her assistance in my trips through the United States, sharing the beauty of the Indian way.

My deep gratitude goes to the writers for being so patient and generous in answering my questions, for their cooperation and friendship. This book is a tribute to all of them.

Introduction

Before we can make valid critical interpretations of the work of American Indian writers, we must consider their tradition and historical background. We need to discover, or rediscover, cultural values other than those rooted in Western aesthetics or in individual aesthetic sensibilities. Therefore my first concern in the interviews gathered here was to provide an adequate cultural perspective, a resource for criticism that would be directly connected to creative activity. The aim of most of the questions I put to the writers was, following the challenge of self-definition so common to writers in postcolonial times, to elicit from them their sense of displacement as well as their sense of belonging, their interpretation of Native Americans in their modern homeland.

On the other hand, it was my intention that all the writers should be given—by means of the interview—the opportunity to discuss a wide sweep of critical issues related to their works, from the interrelation among different Native American cultures to the links between past and present at work in the creative process, from the Native American contribution to contemporary fiction and poetry (of which, of course, Indian literature is an intrinsic part) to the possible influence exerted by Anglo-American authors on indigenous writers.

The interview-conversation format seemed to be particularly appropriate to get into the writers' workshops, their personal recollections and ideas, in the most direct way, without any mediation or disguise. And the interview as a form of autobiography, as a form of orality, can be rightly placed—in its modern structure—in the tradition of the Indian cultural world.[1]

Thus I began my physical journey, meeting the writers at their permanent residences or reaching them where they were at that moment (for they do indeed travel extensively). I asked questions, listened to their answers, and listened also to their manner of speaking and telling, as they chiseled images and concepts out of words with the very special talent their people have for this art.

Their voice of protest, of resistance, of literary creativity, has only in recent times begun to receive much attention from the reading public and literary critics. If we ask ourselves, more than twenty years after the publication of the Pulitzer Prize–winning novel *House Made of Dawn* (1968) by N. Scott Momaday, who these writers are and how they write, the answer is first and foremost that the achievement of a whole generation stems from their declaration of cultural independence. Indian novelists and poets tell a story of their own with no parallel in world literature.

Memory, language, and storytelling tradition—so closely intertwined—are crucial to them. Their personal and historical recollections map distinctive identities conveyed through a powerful language. Words, then, are not mere referents, they are life-giving. To use language is literally to create: "we imagine ourselves, we create ourselves, we touch ourselves into being with words"; "Language is a way of life. . . . by language we create knowledge." Momaday points to the ethics of the word born of an oral tradition. The word is a means of knowledge and experience, and it stands at the core of community life, reflecting the ultimate act of sharing: "It seems to me that in a certain sense we are all made of words; that our most essential being consists in language. It is the element in which we think and dream and act, in which we live our daily lives. There is no way in which we can exist apart from the morality of a verbal dimension."[2]

And imagination shapes new dimensions from the old. Stories from the past merge with the present, ever changing in their structural dynamics, ever the same in their unending continuity in tradition. Not surprisingly, narrative architecture often takes the form of a circular progression, as an ongoing concept rather

than a geometrical design; the ending coincides with a new beginning, mingling history and contemporary events in the communal act of storytelling.

One may ask whether something has been lost in the passage from the oral to the written form, whether the two share
a common source, and what they share. Momaday finds a common denominator in the fact that "the writer like the storyteller
. . . is concerned to create himself and his audience in language." Simon Ortiz believes that "writing . . . is the utilization
of language, and 'the utilization of language' means referring to
the oral tradition."[3] As for using English—the language of the
dominant culture—it means that yet another language has been
acquired by a people who were multilingual before European
colonization.

Seeking the common source, Momaday states that the very
origin of American literature lies in the landscape of America:
"I have an idea that American literature really begins with the
first human expression of man in the American landscape, and
who knows how far back that goes; but it certainly antedates
writing, and it probably goes back a thousand years or more. So
we have to admit it now, and always think in terms of it. We
cannot think of Melville without thinking of American Indian
antecedents in the oral tradition, because the two things are not
to be separated logically at all."[4]

Deeply rooted in the past, as well as in contemporary social
realities, Native American literature portrays characters in quest
of a modern identity. It shows the strife and wonder of their
search and discoveries. It is innovative and stimulating, rich
with suggestions and easily distinguished for its integrity amid
the recurrence of "white shamanism"—a term which denotes
the recycling of native materials by white writers who assume
shamanic status and pass off their derivative work as "native"
American literature.

A variety of illuminating answers, covering a broad range
of topics, emerge from the interviews, but they cluster in
three groups: the first concerns peculiarities inherent in Native
American literature; the second pertains to the writer and his
readership; the third focuses on the writer and his work.

Tribal background, for example, is either carefully described or inferred when these writers talk about their work. As Paula Gunn Allen—a formidable Native American critic—points out, geographic origins explain differences in personalities and affect both the delineation of fictional characters and the elaboration of themes. Native American literature has, then, to be seen as multiethnic.

In these writers a rich tribal heritage fosters a sense of Pan-Indianness. But the sense of unity in the achievement of mutual goals does not mean becoming less tribal, as Wendy Rose explains: "To be tribal and to be Pan-Indian exist side by side, and in fact Pan-Indianism is intended to protect those tribal identities, not to replace them."[5]

Central to most contemporary Native American works, as the writers state in the interviews, are the mixed-blood Indians, characters not previously portrayed by Native American writers in American literature. For white nineteenth-century writers, mixed-bloods were a cultural projection of the American frontier. Their noble, or ignoble, Indians embodied either the opposition of wilderness and civilization or the sentimental integration of two races. In the works of such writers, in fact, just as full-bloods had no remarkable place in prehistory and no place at all in history, mixed-bloods melted into the contemporary white background. No matter how historical and social perspectives have varied over the past hundred years, in mainstream American literature the real problems posed by mixed-bloods have been ignored. But in Native American contemporary writing, mixed-bloods are reborn to dig out their roots, no longer an ambiguous cultural symbol or, as Wendy Rose says, "a biological thing" but "a condition of history, a condition of context, a condition of circumstance . . . a political fact."[6] And in some recent novels their reaffirmation in history means that mixed-bloods are able to reestablish relationships with the land: this "appropriation" of the North American continent, this unique experience, is "a very great investment, a kind of spiritual investment in the landscape," as Momaday calls it.[7] It is the first and most important step toward the acquisition of a new identity.

Among the ten writers interviewed, six are women. Indeed they play a unique role in current Native American literature.

In creation myths and in the storytelling tradition, women have been repositories and transmitters of culture. The same can be said for contemporary women, who maintain vital connections from one generation to the other, even though the loss of traditional ways has been devastating and the pressures toward acculturation are always at work, to the extent that Linda Hogan says, "It's almost as if we have to reeducate ourselves to be families again, to be mothers."[8] That women have always held important positions in various tribal communities disproves Western, patriarchal stereotypes according to which women are inferior to men in a warrior-dominated society.

American Indian women's literary production covers a whole gamut of experiential and emotional landscapes: the interrelation between traditional values and new lifestyles, the development of the artist, the difficult and complicated relationship with feminism and white women's organizations. The sense of wholeness, which women represent metaphorically or in recurring images (and about which women writers are asked in the interviews), speaks of continuity, self-definition, and universal cosmologies as opposed to cultural disintegration.

Two hotly debated issues concerning anthropologists and non-Indian critics are discussed by the writers. In the interviews there emerges a strong critique of those anthropologists who failed in many instances to interpret Native American culture correctly, succumbing as they often did to the bias and myths of a science invented by Western colonialism.

As for non-Indian critics of Native American literature, the writers maintain that critics' work can be good but at times not very constructive, especially if it does not enlarge the writer's view, or if it is off target. Excessive praise or a negative attitude can be as much an impairment as a limited perspective. Among other things, looking at Native American writers means looking at the Native American people and at all they stand for in the United States. A different background and education can drastically affect a critic's ability to understand the Indian cultural world, and even to understand to what extent his or her own approach to Native American literature has been conditioned, despite good intentions and sympathetic feelings.

However, as pointed out in the interviews, a literary movement needs critics, and an increasing number of the most intelligent and dedicated ones are training new scholars. Their work has been crucial in bringing Native American literature into greater circulation and opening up debate. The already impressive amount of scholarship is something one may honestly and respectfully argue with.

Perhaps the work of the critics could be viewed as still in the process of assessing a complex, ongoing literature for which an interdisciplinary approach seems more than ever appropriate. Setting the work in the proper context, developing a critical understanding and what may be called a tribal aesthetics, also implies following a dynamic and multicultural method which is at the base of every critical effort.

The delicate relationship between writers and critics has encountered another area of disagreement: the constant publication of significant works by Native American writers in the past few decades has been considered a "renaissance." However, some of the writers do not accept that term as applied to this flourishing literary production. They maintain that the enduring vitality of the oral tradition has been central to every form of expression, and as Simon Ortiz argues, "in that sense the literature has always been there; it just hasn't been written, with its more contemporary qualities and motives."[9] More than that, as already noted, "working with words" is a traditional Indian value.

Even though this literature is also considered by the Indian audience as a means of survival, publishing is still not always easy for contemporary Native American writers: Linda Hogan explains, "I think it's easier for a non-Indian to write a book about Indian people and get it published than it is for us. Our own experiences and our own lives don't fit the stereotypes."[10] Both the publishing industry and the reading public at large are still influenced by the images of Indians spread by the media. But important literary prizes accorded to Indian writers in the past few years have helped them to reach the mass market. And the work still in progress referred to by these writers confirms that much more will be achieved. The body of literature which will see print in the near future explores new creative possibilities.

By challenging the relationship between writer and reader, this literature, it is hoped, will develop an even more stimulating critical readership.

All the writers I selected for my project are major, productive authors; from this point of view, in fact, others could be included. But because of the growing number of Native American writers in the literary world, I was compelled to make some choices. So as to offer a wide spectrum of Indian cultural heritage, I made my selection according to such considerations as tribal background and geographical place of origin. The areas I chose—the Southwest, Northwest, Plains, and Midwest—are of great interest because they stand for the history of the Indian in the United States and they offer different interpretations of the spirit of place.

Since there are outstanding authors both in fiction and poetry, I have included an equal number of novelists and poets. Although some of them are both, Paula Gunn Allen, Linda Hogan, Joy Harjo, Simon Ortiz, and Wendy Rose are mainly known as poets. Furthermore, to take into account the literary achievements of Indian women writers, I included six among the most acclaimed women writers who also fit well into my selection regarding background, geographical area, and literary genre.

Of interest to me also were the recurring themes in Native American literature, and some of them are particularly evident in certain authors: the interpretation of the trickster character in Gerald Vizenor and Ortiz, or the mixed-blood in Rose, for example, have peculiarities of their own. Then the great popularity of a very young writer, Louise Erdrich, aroused my interest in her talent with respect also to the creative process she shares with her husband, Michael Dorris.

It was my wish to interview all the writers at one single period and literary climate so that a common cultural milieu could be seen. Fortunately I was successful in doing this, thanks to the writers' cooperation.

The interviews took place in houses, restaurants, gardens, motel rooms. I followed no precise format, but I did have two sets of questions, all of which were asked in one continuous meeting. One set of questions was specific for each writer; the other dwelt on issues of interest to the whole group. With the latter set I hoped to form a sort of writers' panel to discuss matters of a general nature.

I let the writers speak for themselves so that the immediacy of the conversational tone would emerge along with the depths, conciseness, and tension of their personal testimony. If their words do ring true, then the difficult task of my remaining unobtrusive will have been transformed into a most rewarding one.

All in all, I hope I have succeeded in making the best possible use of the interviewing instrument and to have been instrumental in "sending a voice" once more.[11]

Paula Gunn Allen

A poet, a novelist, and a critic, Paula Gunn Allen is one of the major figures in American Indian literature. Born in 1939 at Cubero, New Mexico, of mixed Laguna, Sioux, and Lebanese descent, she holds B.A., M.F.A., *and* PH.D. *degrees and has received a National Endowment for the Humanities Creative Writing Fellowship and many other awards. She has taught at San Francisco State University, at the University of New Mexico, and at Fort Lewis College, Durango, California. Her first books of poetry include* The Blind Lion *(1974),* Coyote's Daylight Trip *(1978),* A Cannon between My Knees *(1981), and* Star Child *(1981). A major publication of poetry,* Shadow Country, *appeared in 1982, followed in 1983 by her first novel,* The Woman Who Owned the Shadows. *Her two most recent poetry collections are* Wyrds *(1987) and* Skins and Bones *(1988).*

Her formidable work as a critic is always accomplished with great originality, reflecting concepts and aesthetic principles particular to Indian culture. In addition to writing numerous articles and essays, Paula Gunn Allen edited Studies in American Indian Literature *(1983), a collection of essays, course designs, and bibliographies that is the standard introduction to the field. She is the author of* The Sacred Hoop: Recovering the Feminine in American Indian Traditions *(1986), a fundamental work for a proper approach to the new literature and for an attentive inquiry into the myths and traditions inherent in the culture of some contemporary authors.*

The mother of three children, Allen is a convinced feminist whose beliefs can be traced back, as she herself states, to the woman-centered pueblo society. Paula Gunn Allen has consistently been very active in American feminist movements as well as in antiwar and antinuclear organizations.

Her joyful exuberance, her intellectual liveliness, and her warmheartedness can all be felt throughout the interview, which took place on March 18, 1985, at her home in San Pablo, California, a small city not many miles from Berkeley, where she teaches in the Native American Studies Program at the University of California.

Rather embarrassed after three hours of conversation, I said, "Sorry, you must be tired, it has been a long interview." "It is also a long trip from Italy," she replied.

LC   In trying to define the dilemma that faces a woman in search of herself, what does it mean nowadays to be an American Indian woman?

ALLEN   I don't know. I was doing a class for a friend of mine, who was teaching on Native American women, and I went and talked about my novel with the class. And a couple of Indian women in the class said to me that I said it's a novel about half-breeds, and they said no, it's about all, all the Indian women, that the conflict as it's developed in the novel is about trying to decide how to be an Indian person. And how to be a modern person. You know these women are in college, or perhaps they work in the cities, or perhaps they try to make a living on the reservation where, as you know, the unemployment rate is terrible—it runs 60 percent or 70 percent. So you can't really stay on the reservation because there are no jobs; there is no money. Most Indian people either live in the city all the time or they go back and forth between the reservation and the city.

So I think that Native American literature is useful to everybody who's trying to move from one world to another. And in America, certainly that's two-thirds of us. And in Europe I'm not sure. But it seems to me that there are many rural populations that have been rural for hundreds and hundreds of years. But the world has changed and so they had somehow come to terms with a whole different technological universe. That's very different from what their families lived in for a long time. And that conflict means How do I keep my sense of what I am? If I am a Native American, how do I stay connected to my tradition, to my language, to my way of seeing the world? And maybe I am the only one in my whole circle and maybe there's ten of us in a big circle of maybe thirty thousand people.

You know, I was thinking yesterday that in this country there are over a million non-Indians to every Indian. So you can see the terms of the difficulty are that no one ever understands you. And if you move away from the old traditions, then your family doesn't understand you either and you don't understand yourself. I am not sure though what it means, except it means to think, and for many people it means to commit suicide, it means to be alcoholic, it means to simply not be able to succeed. But for many of us—some forty thousand American Indian women have advanced degrees—it means being in the professions; it means finding ways to link up the different parts of ourselves and the different parts of our lives—to raise children, to be urban, to be rural, and to maintain some sense of who we are. And it's not easy. Because nobody around you understands what that means, what who I am means. So it's a constant fight to keep in mind for yourself who you are. And that's not all bad.

LC   How did the acculturation change American Indian women's lifestyle?

ALLEN   It shifted us from women-centered cultures or cultures that had high respect for women to the position of—the loss of status is so great, it's so great I can barely begin to talk about it. It's hard enough to talk about it; it's almost impossible to find hard evidence, though more is coming to the surface all the time. And then the whole establishment, the anthropologists, the folklorists, the missionaries, and then finally in the past twenty or thirty years, the Indian people themselves have lost all notion of what the status has been. But battery against women is just horrifying—and rape. And those two things tell more about what's happened to the status of women in three hundred years or five hundred years than anything else I can think of.

So what happened was we went from a position of real respect in individual cultures, whether they were women centered or not women centered, to a position of—the bottom, the pits. And it gets worse and worse all the time. It's economic, it's social, it's familiar, it's in every kind of respect. One thing I know is that you can find out two things about a person, an Indian person, about how traditional they are. If they haven't respect for women they've lost the tradition—I don't care how well they speak Indian—they have lost something that's in their hearts or that should be inside them. That and their [hostile] attitude toward homosexuality. These two things will tell me more about how acculturated they are than anything I can think of. But it's dreadful, it's just dreadful. And I have applied several times to get money to detail this shift in status and I can't get the money, because no one wants to hear it. And right now, in my lifetime, we've gone through that shift in the West. And we could document it. It would take a lot of money to do it, but if I could just spend one year interviewing people in different tribes, I could get a lot of information. But I can't get the money to do it. They'll pay me to write about Indian novels, but they don't want me to write about Indian women. And that says something, says something terribly important.

LC   Are Indian women active in women's organizations?

ALLEN   No—no. There are some Indian women's organizations, Women of All Red Nations and a few others. There are a few, a very few medicine societies. And there are women now who are taking part in tribal council and tribal government. But that's not the same thing as women who are feminists. Of course, you understand if there are a million non-Indians to one Indian, our presence is never going to be tremendously visible. But still, feminism for American Indian women is a very difficult thing, and I would guess that maybe 10 percent or less of all American Indian women are even remotely concerned with it.

LC   But it has been said that for American Indian women feminism is synonymous with heritage. Do you agree?

ALLEN   I believe that. That's why I am a feminist. Because I don't see any contradiction between feminism and my tribal background. I think the two are the same thing. But because of patriarchal politics, because of Christianization, because of the terrible, terrible degradation of American Indian women, because they are

Paula Gunn Allen

trained to believe by their families and, more importantly, by the
younger men around them—not the older men but the younger
men—that they are betraying their people if they join with feminism, it's very difficult, very difficult.

Then on top of it, you get into some women's movement
group and they cannot understand what Indian means, and so
they keep objectifying it in ways that are terribly painful. So
women I've known who were active in the women's movement,
Indian women I've known who were active, have very often quit
and gone home because they couldn't deal with it. You know,
you expect a sisterhood to be sisterhood. And it isn't. And what
you have to learn is that nothing's perfect. And we need to be in
there affecting the women's movement because it's our survival,
not just ours as women, but ours as tribal people. Because without that element of respect for women, there's no tribe. There
may be some folks dancing around in feathers and talking funny,
but there's no tribe. It's lost. And some people understand that,
but a lot of people don't.

LC   Can you see any difference in the way the American Indian male
and the female writers choose and develop themes, characters,
events?

ALLEN   It's complicated, it's not simple. For one thing, if they are drawing from tribal traditions, the men are going to draw from male
tribal traditions and the women are going to draw from female
traditions. That's because the tribes have always been sex-segre-
gated in certain ways. So many rituals and parts in rituals are
gender specific. So if you're drawing from ritual or from the oral
tradition or from folklore, the women are going to draw from one
set of symbols and narrative structures and the men are going
to draw from another one. Now, everybody else in the world
doesn't understand that. So if you say "Indian" they kind of expect it—a poem, for instance—to be about hunting, and if it's
a woman's poem it should be about babies. No, no, no, no, no.
The women's sphere is not confined simply to babies and men-
struation. It's many, many, many things: agriculture, building
houses as well as keeping them, creativity in every conceivable
respect you can think of, intellectualism, philosophy. But it will
be different from the men's way of doing those things. So what

you'll notice, if you read the women and the men, is a very real difference in preoccupation and theme. You'll notice some similarities—they are both spiritual, they are both very inclined to use a lot of, let's call it, natural imagery, although the imagery is not used the same way as romantic poets use it. They are inclined to speak about the family and about the tribe and about Indian people—powwows and things like that, you know. So they'll do those things in common. But they'll have very specific preoccupations, and those preoccupations, or perspectives, will show up in structures as well as in the content.

LC   You have called yourself a "multicultural event" who "can attest to the terrible pain of being a bridge" and at the same time "the strength and clarity of commitment and vision that such a heritage engenders."[1] Would you speak about your family background?

ALLEN   Well, my mother is a Laguna, but she's a half-breed. And not only is she a half-breed, her grandfather was a Scotch-American. They have been in this country for five generations, I think. And then her grandmother was a full-blood Laguna woman, but they were Presbyterians. But Grandma always went to the dances and she'd take my mother with her. Then later my mother's mother married a man, an immigrant from Germany, a Jew. And my mother is able to speak English and Mexican Spanish interchangeably and read and write both languages. Then when she married my father, she became a Roman Catholic. So we were raised Catholic. But next door to us, my grandmother was Presbyterian and Indian, and my grandfather was a German Jew. Now, my father's family is of Lebanese extraction. His father was born in Lebanon; his mother was born in Lebanon. My father was born in the United States, but he was born in Seboyeta, which is a Mexican land-grant village north of Laguna Pueblo, and he didn't speak English until he was nine or ten. He spoke Spanish and Arabic. And he was raised Roman Catholic because there was no Maronite rite in New Mexico at the time and that was the closest they could get. And so he was raised Roman Catholic, but in a Spanish-speaking village. So my relatives speak Arabic, English, Laguna, German, Spanish. And their religions are Presbyterianism and Lutheranism because my mother's father's sister-in-law was Lutheran and they also lived in Cubero. Well, there's Protestant, Catholic, and Indian, all in the family as religions, all of those languages, plus my family has a habit of marrying out. So I have Italian relatives, Swedish relatives, Salvadoran relatives, Jewish relatives, Anglo relatives. Just people from everywhere are related to me by blood, and so that's why I say I'm a multicultural event. Because I had to grow up being able to deal with all those different culture styles. It's beautiful, it's a rainbow. It really is. And I can't think of anything more beautiful than a rainbow. It reflects light, and I think that's what a person like me can do. Or we can feel persecuted and oppressed and victimized, and then what? And we go shoot ourselves or something. And that doesn't make any sense. And I think in some respects the whole world is a multicultural event, and it's possible, if it's possible for me to stay alive, then it's possible for the whole world to stay alive. If I can communicate, then all the different people in the world can communicate with one another.

LC   Speaking about Native Americans as a people, you can't identify a national background in terms of a unified common culture, language, tribal heritage, and so on. Do you see, then, American Indian literature as a multiethnic literature?

ALLEN   Absolutely. The study I'm working on now is detailing the tribal elements in, I think, seven novels. And to do that I have to look specifically at the author's tribe and also at the tribe the author is drawing from because [N. Scott] Momaday, for instance, uses Kiowa, Navajo, and Jemez, but he's Kiowa mostly. So I have not only to look at his background but also at the traditions he's drawing from. And that novel [*House Made of Dawn*] in itself is a multicultural novel, right there. But all of them are that way. So I'm doing [James] Welch and Louise Erdrich and Gerald Vizenor. There are two Chippewas, or Anishinabeg, now, Erdrich and Vizenor, and then there are three southwestern novelists—I call us "The Magical Mystery Tour"—Leslie Silko, me, and Momaday, and then two northwestern writers, D'Arcy McNickle and Mourning Dove. And it happens that Okanagans and the Flatheads are approximately the same people—they are very close. And since they are from approximately the same area as the Blackfeet and Gros Ventre, their novels connect with the novels of James Welch. So what I can do is I can put these works together and I can analyze that cultural diversity. So you can see that these are specific things that go on for Anishinabeg that are not going to go on for Lagunas and that are not going to go on for the Salish. Isn't that nice? We have enough novels now, so I can do that.

LC   Do American Indian writers have a large audience among Indian people?

ALLEN   It's growing. It's growing.

LC   Do Indian people see the writer's work as a means to preserve their culture?

ALLEN   Ten years ago I would have said no. Three years ago I would have said no. But now I say, yes, we do. And it's thrilling. Several writers and I were at Haskell Institute, an Indian community college in Kansas; it's an old, old Indian school, and the people there, the staff, were saying, "Oh, well, probably no one will come. Well, we're glad you're here, but don't be too upset if the students don't turn out." Well, they were hanging from the roof. There were students everywhere. And they stayed for two days. They listened to the readings, they listened to the papers, the scholarly presentations. There was a flute player who came along; oh, it was beautiful, and he lectured on the flute and then he played. It was just incredible. Hundreds, hundreds of youngsters and in that time I was there I met two young geniuses and one very competent poet. And I didn't talk to very many people.

There are many Indian libraries, and the students write and ask for books or ask for bibliographies. I'm going up to Humboldt State [University] next month to read for Indian Awareness Week. And what I'm saying is that we're so new. The fact that Native American people have writers of their own is so new that it's taken awhile, but we're beginning to have a real effect. We're beginning to take control of the image making again. And that's what most happens, because whoever controls your definition controls your sense of self. And so the more writers we have and the more readers we have and audience we have, the more Native American people are going to be able to claim themselves, and take it back from Hollywood, take it back from the anthropologists. Isn't that exciting? There are only a million Indians in this country; when we are talking about audience one has always to be aware what that means. But we have a good one.

LC   Does literature develop a sense of Pan-Indianness?

ALLEN   Yes, yes, it tells us who we are; it tells us what our history is; it tells us what we look like; and it tells us of the significance of our lives within the human community. It takes us out of the realm of oblivion, which is where we've been. If we live in the past, and by 1850 it's all over, you know what that tells a young Indian person? It tells a young Indian person you died in 1890, so what are you doing here? Now we can say, look what you're doing here, look at this literature, it's so fine, it's superb literature, and they can read it and they can say—I got some letters back from those students and they were saying—"it's so wonderful to listen to our own—it's like listening to ourselves. It's like hearing who we are and feeling comfortable and going 'oh, I recognize that.'" Now instead of having to strain and understand when you're reading a poem by an English poet—well, what do we know about England? it's an exotic place to me—instead I can read about Cubero, I can read about Laguna, I can read about Jemez. I know these places, I know the landscape, I know the people, I know the sounds. I know, I understand. It's giving us our sanity back, person by person, and tribe by tribe. In a way we all died, but we're still here. And the literature allows us to come to terms with both facts. Because both things are true. The women, by the way, are better at that than men. The women are really good at dealing with continuance, at holding on. The men are better at dealing with war and death. But that's because the men's traditions are about war and death and women's traditions are about continuance. That seems to be pretty true tribe by tribe all over the country, by the way, and that's interesting.

LC   As you said in "The Trick Is Consciousness," [*Coyote's Daylight Trip*], "In the silence of recovery we hold / the rituals of the dawn / now as then."

ALLEN   That's right. That's where we're at. Recovery.

LC   An interesting point you make in one of your articles is that the conflicts of the main characters in *House Made of Dawn* [Momaday], *Ceremony* [Silko], *Winter in the Blood* [Welch], and *The Death of Jim Loney* [Welch] are resolved variously according to

the geographical area the authors come from. Can you discuss
that further?

ALLEN   Let's see. Okay. Jim Loney dies a warrior's death. That's very
clear. *Holca hoka hey, hey;* "it is a good day to die." The reason
it's a warrior's death is because it's on Indian land, it's in the
mountains, his enemy—his honorable enemy—kills him, and
because he chooses his death. That's what's the most important
thing. He's not a victim. In the end he's no longer a victim. He
defines himself, and that's what's terribly important there. In
House Made of Dawn Abel spends his whole life trying to cope
with the fact of who he is and isn't. And that witchcraft and
ritual are the same thing. He can't get that. It's so hard for him to
understand that. Witchcraft is what Christians say you've been
doing when you are doing something they don't understand. It's
ritual. But by the time Abel is born both of those ideas are in
the pueblo. So the Pueblo people themselves don't understand
witchcraft and ritual. And they don't understand that there isn't
really a difference. Because Christians have been with them for
hundreds of years. There's historical documentation on how this
shift goes. Anyway, so what Abel has to learn is that ritual is
his life. And that it's not about who's good and who's bad; it's
about what your obligation is. And obligation to your people
after death, for the Pueblos, is at least as important as obligation
to your people before death. So of course Abel has to run into
the dawn after his physical death, and he must perform his obligations to the living after death. Because that's what a Pueblo
has to do. It's a rule. So that's how he resolves his crisis. It's
by falling into the tradition in terms of serving after he's gone.
Whereas Loney follows the tradition by defining the time and
place of his death, which is a very Plains thing to do.

What Leslie [Silko] does is interesting. She writes a novel
[*Ceremony*] all about the feminization of a male. That's really
what it's about. And the ideal for a Laguna or an Acoma male is
that he learn how to be a woman. That's because at those pueblos
God is a woman. And the important deity besides Thinking
Woman is Iyatiko, Earth Woman, Corn Woman; and so in order
for the land to be balanced and the people to be happy, all the
people, men and women alike, must learn to nurture and to

think more about peace and harmony and prosperity, making things grow, taking care of things, then they never think about destruction and self-indulgence and personal emotions, none of which matter. What matters is that the people stay, and that we all live. That's what's important. And that the land be healthy so that she can bear. So that's how Leslie resolves the crisis. Once again, she pulls Tayo, the protagonist, back into the tradition. And he's an outsider, but he's not an outsider physically because he always moves in the direction of Pueblo manhood, which is to walk in balance in a mothering sense or, shall I say, the feminine sense. Not that he's got to wear skirts and lipstick, but that he has to learn how to nurture, how to be a mother. That's what he has to learn, so that's what she writes about.

Welch's *Winter in the Blood*, as near as I can tell, is some sort of an initiation book. It's about Blackfeet, and it's about how a man finds his name. He's not a man until he goes through a certain series of spiritual and personal events out of which comes his identity. That's an old tradition. His novel is not about simply living in the modern world. It's about living in the modern world because you can't walk that traditional path here in modern America as easily as you could walk it in the traditional world of five hundred years ago or so. And what he's saying is that the traditions will transpose into another key and they won't lose their integrity. You can take the same tradition, put it into a new context, the context that you live in, and you can still fulfill your traditional obligations which really, in some sense, is what all those novels are saying.

LC   In many American Indian novels, short stories, and poems, humor is central to the real essence of the story itself, it almost shapes its structure and gives full meaning—otherwise hidden or misinterpreted—to characters and event. Is there a difference in the use of humor in the old Indian stories and in the contemporary ones?

ALLEN   It's more bitter in the contemporary ones. It's almost gallows humor. Sometimes it's exactly that, whereas in the earlier stories it's much more direct and much more clear. I'll say pure, but I don't mean innocent and simpleminded and silly. I mean that, when you've gone through five hundred years of genocidal experiences, when you know that the other world that surrounds you wants your death and that's all it wants, you get bitter. And you don't get over it. It starts getting passed on almost genetically. It makes for wit, for incredible wit, but under the wit there is a bite. It's not defensive so much as it's bitter. It also makes for utterly brilliant, tragic writing as well. Because it's so close to the bone. It's not some middle-class person sitting around imagining what it would be like to be in trouble. It's about your own life. Your own and your mother's and your sister's and your nephew's and your uncle's and everybody's. It's real life. And so when you laugh you know perfectly well that you're laughing at death. Real death.

I often think that if the people who are into survival, you know, the antinuclear people, if they really understood extinction, they would have a kind of strength and lucidity that they don't have, at least not in this country. Because in this country, Americans don't really understand what real death might mean. Europeans understand it. They just went through it twice. They know. And Indians in this country, we know because we had it happen recently. I mean it's not as though it was five hundred years ago. It's a continuing process because they're always trying to kill the Indian. They are always trying to completely obliterate Indianness. You can never escape knowing that.

So there's this tradition of humor, of an awful lot of funniness, and then there's this history of death. And when the two combine, you get a power in the work; that is, it moves into another dimension. It makes it transformational. It creates a metamorphosis in the reader, if the reader can understand what's being said and what's not being said. And that's the hard part, of course, for non-Indians. It's hard for them to understand the terms of the dialogue that's going on between the writer and his or her fundamental community. Because that's where we're writing from, you know; it's the dialogue between "I" and "we" that's going on in the work.

LC Starting from the end of the last century, many anthropologists transcribed and then translated chants, legends, creation stories, from Indian informants giving oral renditions. Quite often, for a variety of reasons, their job has not done justice to the meaning

Paula Gunn Allen

or technique of oral literature. Your uncle, John Gunn, transcribed Keres legends in *Schat-chen* [1917]. What do you think of it?

ALLEN   I wrote a paper called "Kochinnenako in Academe" that was published in the *North Dakota Quarterly* in 1985 and will be in my new book, *The Sacred Hoop: Recovering the Feminine in American Indian Traditions* [1986]. I talked about exactly what I think on the matter of translation. It's very complicated. People who were raised at Laguna, in the language, tell me that the book is true, but it's funny. It's like it's upside down. It's not wrong. He [John Gunn] is not in error, but he does something funny with the book. Well, the funny thing he does is that he looks at it out of a Euro-American perceptual frame of context. So when he hears the stories, he hears them this way. So you get things like the "Ruler's Daughter." The ruler's daughter? What ruler? There is no ruler. And it's sort of like the princess and the prince. It's all very European folktale. Of course, if he's going to translate a legend, he's going to put it in the paradigm that makes sense to him. Not only that, but he got a certain number of those stories from my grandmother, who became his wife in their later years. He lived with his brother and his brother's wife. They were family. His brother's wife used to tell me stories when I was little, and she would translate them into what she thought were American images. So when she wanted to talk about Navajos, she called them gypsies because she thought, these people are in wagons and would wear beautiful clothes. And the Navajos and Pueblos don't get along too well. So that was an accurate translation, if you understand what she was doing.

Or when she would talk about the spirit people she would call them fairies. Well, they're similar to me. But if you don't know what she's doing, it really messes it up. So what Uncle John did —he spoke the language well—was just sit and visit with people. And he didn't go around trying to be the great anthropologist. He'd just sit and visit. He'd listen. And then he'd translate from the Laguna, which he spoke, not only into English but into Western thought, and that's what causes the thing to turn upside down. Many times he didn't know that the story he was hearing was connected to a ritual, and since he never attended the dances or anything—I mean, he was really good, he was really polite and respectful—he didn't know how to put it into a framework.

Still, I'll bet you that he's done some of the best work that's ever been done. Because he didn't try to mess with it. He did innocently mess with it, but because he's innocent it's fairly easy to untangle what he's done. And because he's not the famous anthropologist, there is no problem to untangle it either; whereas if he were Franz Boas and you say, hey, this guy's got it wrong, why all of the intellectuals of the world would rear up and say, "Well, how can you say such a thing?" And of course you can say such a thing. There's another problem, and that is that the Pueblos themselves don't like to talk about any of these things.

LC   Are you talking about creation stories?

ALLEN   Above all creation stories because they are not stories. They're sacred power. And it's like the deep secrets of the Vatican. The Pueblos don't talk about that either. And that's how it is when you're dealing with sacred mysteries. You don't talk about them. And also their world is so different, so—it's so completely different from the Western world that even if they would talk about it, you couldn't understand it. Even if you tried very, very hard to get it exactly right, it's not going to translate. So the best you can do is translate intuitively and then readers have to read intuitively because there is no other way to do it.

LC   You have to get the feeling of it.

ALLEN   That's right. And some sense. And to do that you have to develop a sensibility. And to do that you have to read and read and read and read. And travel and meet people and talk to people.

LC   What about E. C. Parson's *Pueblo Indian Religion* [1939]?

ALLEN   Actually that's a book I haven't spent any time with, so I won't even try to comment on it. But I read her *Laguna Genealogies*. And that other work, *Notes on Ceremonialism at Laguna* [1920]. And they're good. They are good.

LC   Good from what point of view?

ALLEN   From a Laguna point of view. The reason they're good is because they make no sense. She has enough sense not to try to make sense. And as a result, you can read between the lines of her work in such a way that you begin to be able to get what goes on there in ways that you can't when the recorder tries to restructure. When Uncle John puts the stuff into a structure, immediately the reader looks at the structure and says, "Oh, I recognize this." And the reader, the Western reader, should not be saying, "I recognize this."

Believe me, if that's what readers are saying, they're making a terrible mistake. And there's something wrong with the text. But what Parsons does, at least in these two monographs that I've looked at, is she gets so completely confused about what's going on, it shows. And as a result, you know that you don't understand and that's the truth. You don't understand. And neither does Ms. Parsons. And that's right, that's true. And so I trust those works because they're confusing. For the other book I don't know. I know that book touched off quite a controversy and it's one of the reasons why the Lagunas closed everything to outsiders because she was using language that's very specific to anthropology and I think that she thought that they didn't know how to read or that they wouldn't read. Well, that was a very foolish mistake on her part. Particularly at Laguna. They're very educated people and they like to read. Okay, so they read it and said, "Oh, good heavens, this woman is making fun of us. She's trivializing us. She's discounting us. She doesn't understand. She's making it all bad. And it's not bad. She's making it sound silly and stupid and trivial." And that's all I can say about it. I don't have any idea what the book says. You know, since I sort of grew up knowing that about the book, I haven't read it.

LC   And just to avoid this lack of Indian perspective do you think then that American Indian anthropologists should collect their own oral literature as Alfonso Ortiz did with Richard Erdoes in the recent *American Indian Myths and Legends*?

ALLEN   Well, he's done a superb job, you know. Because he knows what he's looking at and he also knows the discipline of anthropology. So what he can do if he's good, and Alfonso's good, he can look at and hold both paradigms in his mind and build a bridge that is now comprehensible to the establishment and at the same time does not distort what he's talking about. He can also respect the barriers. All he has to say is "this we don't talk about," and let it go at that. And in that way he's not offending the people he's drawing from. And at the same time he's not distorting either. If the area is closed, it's closed. That's that. But he can still tell you what the structures are and you can then get some clear sense. This is difficult. Ella Deloria did a superb job too in her *Dakota Texts* [1939]. The problem that is endemic to the situation is that the discipline of anthropology recruits Indians into the program to teach them to be sophisticated informants, not to teach them to be sophisticated theoreticians. So what happens is that you get a sort of unintellectualized servant class; that's what we're supposed to be for the white man, the servant class. And this works out in anthropology, as well as it works out in Carlisle Indian School or Haskell or someplace. And so the Indian people who're going to go into anthropology have got to pay attention to the fact they are going to be used, and that they mustn't allow that to happen. They need to learn to be competent theoreticians as well as competent researchers. And then not to be used, get the PH.D. and then go to do some real work. And that's all I want to see happen.

LC   What can you say about publishing the works by American Indian writers, about small presses and well-known publishers such as Harper and Row and its series devoted to American Indian writers?

ALLEN   Harper and Row. I sent Harper and Row my novel for their feminist series, and they really liked it. The editors really liked it a lot. But they decided to reject it on the grounds that white feminists wouldn't read it. Guess who published the book. White feminists published the book. Guess who read the book. White feminists read the book. Well, this just leads me into what I'm about to say. The publishing industry is about twenty years behind the reading public. That's the problem. If the publishers actually knew what's going on in the readership. It's money but it's not money. They're losing money. See, they think that they're making money and they're saving money. No, no, no, no, no. They're losing money. Because I was raised as a business person. My father's a merchant. Also I am a Lebanese. And what I know about business is that you meet the demand. You don't pretend that everybody wants to eat something twenty years old when they are looking for something right now. If you want to make money, then you find out what they want. And then you give it to them because you can make more money that way.

It's because publishing is specialized. If you teach at Berkeley, pretty soon you don't know anything else exists on earth except Berkeley. Well, if you work at a publishing house, pretty soon you don't know anything else exists except what the staff talks about. And the publishing industry is very ingrown. I mean these people all talk to each other. They don't talk to anybody else, only to each other. They work in these tall high-rise buildings that you can't get into without passing thirty security checks. I mean, where do they live? They don't live anywhere the readers live. So, of course, it's natural for them to make mistakes. There's something deeper though that's more of a problem. And that is that they, like the larger American public, have some strange ideas about what is Indian. And they will not easily allow publications by people who don't fit their preconception. But the preconception was created by dime novels. By writers like James Fenimore Cooper, Daniel Defoe, and such, and by Hollywood: in fact, one of the first movies made before the talkies was some Indian story. One of those horrible, treacherous Red Man sort of movies about George Custer, on TV now. And everybody in this country thinks they know what Indian is, when mostly they know what the media thinks it is. And that goes for the Indian people as well as for the non-Indian people. The first thing that happens to an immigrant who comes over here is she's sitting up watching late-night TV and she learns all about Indians in John Wayne movies. So of course it's very difficult for us to publish unless we act like "proper" Indians.

Jamake Highwater acts like a proper Indian, whether he's Indian or not. He gets all the coverage because he acts like you're supposed to act if you want to dance to the white man's Indian music. I find that offensive, humiliating, and dangerous. It's not good for people to act like that. It's not good for them to degrade themselves that way. They'll wind up dead. They musn't do it. And if you can't get published, then the heck with it. Too bad. But you can't sell your soul. Unfortunately the people who know how to play media Indian get a lot more goodies than people who don't. There are some exceptions, thank heaven, but I look at my little list of our novels, maybe fifteen altogether, then I look at the list of black novels; it's really depressing. It's not that we can't write. We can write. It's not that we don't know. We do know. It's not that we don't have wonderful stories to tell. We do. It's that there's nobody there to hear them. Linda Hogan has a line [in "Blessing," *Calling Myself Home* (1978)] that I quote all the time. It goes: "Blessed/are those who listen/when no one is left to speak." And that's sort of what has almost happened to us—that there are those who would listen but there is nobody who could speak. Because they won't let us speak. But that's okay, we speak anyway. But let me say one more thing about that. I don't want to sound absolutely depressed and discouraged because really that's not fair, or exactly accurate. Since 1968, since *House Made of Dawn*, we are publishing a fair amount. We're publishing more than I can keep up with. I finally had to specialize because we now have more literature than I can deal with easily. And well, you wait till 2050, we'll be one of the major forces in the literary world. I'll lay you odds. Isn't it [César] Vallejo who was a surrealist? But he was from Peru. He was a half-breed. And he had such an important impact on James Welch, who was also interested in the surrealist movement. The thing is, he was not a surrealist, he was an Indian—which is mentioned, but not perceived as a cultural and literary influence on his writing. Look at the impact that he had on world literature. Well, it'll be like that too for any number of writers now and in fifty years.

LC   What do you think of the white readers and critics of your work and of American Indian literature in general?

ALLEN   Sometimes critics are very good; sometimes the lack of information is depressing. Everybody, or almost everybody, is well intentioned, sympathetic. They want to understand and they don't understand the degree to which they've been conditioned to think certain thoughts and to not think others. But I long for the day when we have critics who are very knowledgeable, because we need that. We, the writers, need that. We need critics who can address specifically what we're doing and not what they wish we had done and not what they imagine we did, but who know what's going on and therefore can make distinctions and illuminations about the literature. But we're developing people like that and there are probably twenty critics in the country who are really good. And they're training new ones. So I don't think it will be too long before I can send out a book and I can trust the reviewers to tell me what I need to know. And I have already got two or three critics that I know I can trust, because they know what I am doing and they know when I fail to do it. And that's what a writer needs; we've got to have that before we can really be a literary movement. We're beginning a literary movement, but we don't quite have all the parts of it yet. We're getting there.

So, as I said, usually it's okay. I get annoyed when Gary Snyder gets a Pulitzer Prize for *Turtle Island* [1974] and Simon Ortiz doesn't get a Pulitzer Prize for *Going for the Rain* [1976]. I mean, that's crazy, crazy thinking. I realize that the Pulitzer committee owed Snyder a Pulitzer for his earlier work, but it's annoying that that's the particular book of his they chose.

I had a review in the *New York Times* for my novel *The Woman Who Owned the Shadows*, and the reviewer wrote a very interesting review, considering that she didn't review the book I wrote. She reviewed the book she imagined I wrote. And she did the same thing to Maxime Hong Kingston's *The Woman Warrior* in the same review. She misunderstood Maxime's book. The reviewers on the East Coast are very important in this country, but people who live in the East don't think the same way as people who live in the West. And in the West, we don't have enough power to make that equal, to make it a dialogue between the two coasts. Right now it's mostly easterners who are the arbiters, whether they know anything about the West or not. And they very often don't. And they very often have never been west of Philadelphia. And so they don't know. And they are truly foreigners. In Europe, one wouldn't expect that somebody who's Italian necessarily can speak to concerns of a French writer unless they're very well trained. In America, if you live in Texas, you know everything there is to know about Maine, and if you live in New York, you know everything there is to know about Laguna. No, no, no, no, no. It doesn't work that way anywhere in the world. Why should it work that way here?

Paula Gunn Allen

In one of your poems, "Los Angeles, 1980," you speak about "the death culture," "the death society," "the dying generation" well dressed in "Jantzen, Wrangler, Gucci and Adidas." Leslie Silko in *Ceremony* speaks about the dissolution of white people's consciousness into dead objects like plastic and neon, the concrete and steel. Is there no way out?

Of their death? They're going to have to die. That's the only way out. And they're busy doing it. Have you noticed? Of course you've noticed. Two massive world wars, a war that's going on now, that's been going on since 1947, since the last one theoretically ended. Death everywhere. You can't turn on the TV without hearing all about the newest death craze, the newest death wave. It's everywhere. So they're doing it. And I am taking that in a spiritual sense. You know, people in the tribal culture don't become full adults until they go through their death trips. It's required of them. And I think that that's what the Western world is doing. It's finally entering its puberty. And all it can do is produce death and contemplate death and think about death. All their literature is about death. At least the literature the critics love, the stuff they give awards to—all their politics is about death. And that's why I call them the death culture. They're obsessed with dying. And now they're very busy having all these nuclear buildups and, with it, nuclear freeze buildups. And both sides are only contemplating death. That's what they're meditating on. That's the whole dialogue now.

Yes there's a way out. That man [Tim Rice] who wrote *Jesus Christ Superstar*—there's a line that I always, always remember. He has Jesus say, "To conquer death, you only have to die." And that's right, that's right. I think there is a way out. You know, when my daughter was thirteen or so, and her brother before her, they went into this sort of re-embryonic phase and they wouldn't open the curtains in their room, and they wanted the room painted dark and their hair in front of their face. And it's sort of normal. And they were rebirthing themselves in some way, and they had to go through all the terrible angst and the depression and horror of adolescence so that they could come out on the other side alive and belonging to themselves, not belonging to me, and not belonging to their fantasies about themselves, and not belonging to their friends, but belonging to themselves. And I think in an individual life that process takes at least fifteen years. We don't get there until we are in our thirties. I didn't. And I don't think anybody else does either. In *Winter in the Blood*, I think that's why the narrator is in his thirties, because he's right at the point where he's going to make the transition into selfhood. And I think that that's what the West is doing.

I've had another poem that goes, "We are the women of the daylight." You know, we wrap ourselves in plastic and cover ourselves with steel, and we got polyester between us and the breath of earth. We always wear shoes so that we can't feel the mother. And that's where we live. But the spirit people are everywhere. I don't care how much they pave it, you can't pave away the spirits. And soon people will recognize that. The Western world will reclaim itself, because it knows this as well as the Indians do. It's just been busy dying. You know, Westerners have died at a greater rate in the past five hundred years than anyone else. You know that. You know what the population of Europe was in 1495 or 1750. So I don't think it's hopeless. It just sounds that way.

LC   As a feminist, do you feel that there is a kind of generation gap between the women's rights movement and the so-called "yuppies"? In other words, what has happened to the younger generation?

ALLEN   I don't know. Probably half of the women I associate with here in the women's community are also yuppies. They're feminist and they're yuppies. And a lot of the yuppies are people who did civil rights work, who did the peace movement, the anti-Vietnam movement, as youngsters. I don't think that there is a generation gap except in the sense that we have a different style. So they're into what they love to call prosperity consciousness. And that's not bad. That's okay. One thing they do is they generate jobs. And they keep a lot of people on the work force who wouldn't have work if the yuppies weren't out there buying everything they could possibly buy. So that's not bad. But they have a different notion. My daughter lives in Marin County and sometimes I look at her and her friends and say, "Is this what I have been working for all these years?" I mean, really! But when

I sit down and talk to them, their understandings are profound; they're deeply spiritual. They're deeply religious. They're deeply engaged in learning self-reliance—and in forming communities that are realistic instead of just woo, woo, sentimental rose-colored-glasses stuff. I think it's the next step in what's going to be a very long march. There's no more gap between them and me than there is between my parents and me. In some ways the gap is unbridgeable, but in some ways we're the same people.

LC   Can you see in your work an evolution concerning themes and style and so on?

ALLEN   I've been entirely preoccupied with colonization for probably all my writing life, and that would be twenty-five years. And metaphorically light and dark, shadows and sun, death and life, and transformation. And now I'm moving much more toward transformation and magic. And not colonization as it's going on so much, but what it brings about, what arises from this phenomenon. I've always been interested in what Elaine Jahner calls mythologizing the cities and finding out where the non-human, the wilderness, dimensions are in the city. Instead of seeing it as a dead thing, seeing it as a live thing. And I'll continue with that, so some of my earlier preoccupations will hang on. I am much more concerned with women, especially with women's ritual and women's spirituality. I'm presently engaged in teaching courses in the old traditions from the Mediterranean, which is my home, as well as this being my home, from all over Europe and the British Isles, and the Americas and Africa and Southeast Asia and India, the world. Finding whatever's left of women's rituals and women's magic and women's religions and women's politics and women's whatever. That's what I probably will be doing for the next twenty years or so. Because it fascinates me, for one thing, and for another, I see very real connections between Central America and the Middle East, the circum-mediterranean countries. I think it's very similar to the culture complex that goes from the Iroquois country, the Great Lakes, all the way around that group in the United States all the way down to the Southwest and around through the Yucatán peninsula, and I think that's all one culture complex: that is, in some sense, mirrored in the circum-mediterranean peoples.

And you can see that's vast and you can see that it can easily preoccupy me for a long time. I'm working on a book about my father's family and I'm working on a novel, a medicine-dyke novel I call it, and I am just finished with *The Sacred Hoop* for Beacon [Press] and I'm working on a research project which is mostly what I'm doing for the grant I got last year. And they all fit together. So I'm interested in transformations, I'm interested in how you go from one phase of being to another phase of being, how you go from one condition or state to another condition or state, which is what ritual is, after all. But I'm getting very real, very detailed, about exactly how that functions and exactly what it is in literature and also in religious structures, religious forms.

LC   Can you describe your writing process?

ALLEN   I sit down at the word processor and off we go. It's really a different process since I got this thing. It's wonderful. I mutter and mumble. I get mad and I clean the house a lot and I pick fights with people. It's terrible! Living with a writer is terrible. I used to live with a writer so I know it's terrible. And then I focus finally and write. I tend to write about three times as much as ever sees print because I'm not good at making outlines. What I am good at is writing. And it's like I get rid of the garbage layer and then I can do the real work. And so then I can pull things from the first twenty pages and then shape the final document that I'm going to have. And so, I waste a lot of paper. And I discover I waste a lot of time, but sitting there writing outlines takes just as much time.

Something I've noticed with *The Sacred Hoop* is that there is what you can call a linear progression of thought as I'm structuring the book, but it's not chronological. So the essays in their chronological order don't have this progression of thought that's clearly a progression. But if I change the order in which you read them, the sequence of them, there is a linear progression of thought. I don't quite understand how that works. I'm going to have to think about that in the next week or so. It's like I have four or five dialogues that I'm carrying on and some of it shows up in an essay on the oral tradition, and some of it shows up in an essay on women, and some of it shows up in a review on somebody's work. It's one thought, but it moves forward by accretion slowly but surely, and it eventually becomes a whole thought, and I think that book will represent a whole thought.

My novel is a thirteen-year conversation, but in the end it represents a whole thought. My writing process also means I have to live the whole thing before I can write it. So I write it in my own life and then I write it on the page. And I suppose that two-thirds of what I live will never get on the page, because there's only so much time to do that. But the process is very complex; it's not just what I sit down and write. It's what I think and what I teach and what I do and who I see and what I feel and who I become. In every sense it's my whole life. And from that I try to select and make coherent. And that's difficult because I know—and according to one ethnologist this is a Laguna trait —I know that nothing's ever simple and that there's more. It's not just that, on the other hand; it's on the other hand, on the other hand, on the other hand, on the other hand. So I could spend the rest of my life trying to write what happened in one week. And I could write fifty books and none of them would be it. Each of them would be about some aspect of it. That's what makes me mumble and makes me irritable. It's because I can't find the one thread that I can follow; writing being what it is, print being what it is and structures being what they are—you can't put everything into it. You have to choose, and trying to figure out what to choose is the hardest part. It keeps me awake at night and it keeps me working in my body and mentally long after I quit working at the word processor, and long before I went to work at it. Because there are so many realities going on at the same time and they're all true. And I don't know how to get that down on the page. I haven't found a form yet. Metaphors are good. The way I structured my novel is good. But there's always something left over that I didn't get in there and I want it in there because I want the truth. And by truth I mean accuracy. I want it to reflect as exactly as it can what it is I'm knowing. That's of course about the craft of writing, and I don't have enough craft. But maybe over the years I'll develop it.

LC And you have a new novel in progress?

ALLEN I sure have. It's called *Raven's Road.*

LC   In your work as a poet, novelist, storyteller, have you been in-
      fluenced by any Anglo-American writer?

ALLEN By Anglo-American and English also. I mean, you can't grow up
      and study literature without doing that. I think a very important
      influence is W. C. Williams and the Black Mountain School of
      poetry, the first exciting writers I found when I decided to write
      poetry. I started out wanting to write fiction. And in fiction,
      when I was little, there was Charlotte Brontë; I read *Jane Eyre*. I
      think I read it twenty times. Also Louisa May Alcott, who had
      me rereading. I don't like to reread books, so it had to be really
      something for me to keep reading it. And Gertrude Stein. I was
      mad for Gertrude Stein in high school. My mother would buy
      me everything she could find, which was not a lot at the time,
      but what she could find. And that sort of sunk in underneath.
      So I think some of the first poems I wrote were very Steinian.
      And that forms part of a structure of my work, because I was
      doing Stein when I was so young. The romantic poets Keats and
      Shelley. I didn't realize this, but my poem "Moonshot, 1969" is
      in some ways a restatement of "Ode to a Nightingale." It was
      quite unconscious. I wasn't thinking of Keats at all. I was trying
      in that poem to write in a voice that Charles Olson has. I love
      that philosophical, sort of dry-as-bones voice.

      And that was what I was trying to do. But I have this roman-
      tic impulse, so it wound up sounding quite a bit like Keats. And
      if you look at the poem, and in "Ode to a Nightingale" the last
      stanza, my last stanza is a paraphrase of his. And I didn't know
      that. But in a dramatic reading program I heard one of the people
      presenting "Ode to a Nightingale" and I almost fell off my chair.
      I didn't read Indian literature, literature made by Indians, until
      House Made of Dawn. And by then I was finishing up my M.F.A.
      in creative writing in Oregon.

      So you see I had no models. There was no such thing as Native
      American writing, contemporary writing, then—not that I knew
      of. When I went to the University of New Mexico, in 1969–70,
      I wanted to fit into English, into the PH.D. program in English,
      and I told the graduate dean that I wanted to focus on Native
      American literature. And he told me there was no such thing,
      which is why I have my degree in American studies. And there

is such a thing now. Whether there was then or not, who cares; there is Native American literature now. So I was heavily influenced by the French writers I've read. I liked Genet and I read everything I could find of his. And Beckett. I like the very cerebral poets. And an American man named Louis Zukofsky and that whole school of writers. I spent hours and hours reading and studying. So those influences are definitely there. I try in a number of poems to structure the poem in a way that's analogous to Mozart's structures in his music. I grew up listening to it. My sister's a musician and she used to sit in our living room in Cubero and we had this big upright piano. And she'd play Mozart and I'd sit in a chair and read and listen to her. And it had a very deep effect on my sense of structure. As a young writer I very consciously worked at trying to find poetic structures that were analogous to those musical structures. A few years ago she analyzed a couple of my poems, that Los Angeles poem was one, she analyzed it as though it were a musical piece. And I did it. I did it. I'm really proud of that.

And then also, all the cowboys. I love cowboys. I love western literature and western music and I grew up listening to that because that's all we got out in Cubero. And that's very important to me. And the church. I grew up a Catholic after all. I sang the mass. Ten different masses I learned to sing. And that's important. There's Arabic rhythms because also there were family gatherings when we'd sing and dance, in Arabic. And those are there. And there's all the Indian stuff I grew up with. Mostly Southwest—Laguna, specifically. I didn't hear any other kind of Indian, anything, until I was over thirty. The first powwow I ever went to, I was in culture shock: What are these people doing? I never saw anything like that. And so, you know, there's very real difference in rhythm, never mind in other things. Like the kinds of rituals and so forth. But there's a very real difference in rhythm between how the Pueblo sing a corn dance and how the Plains, say, sing a fast fancy dance. You could hear the differences. So the influences are multitudinous.

I like popular literature. I'm one of those people who would read almost anything. You know, stuff on packages. Anything. But my mother would try to get me to read Charles Dickens

—I couldn't read Charles Dickens! She'd try to get me to read George Eliot and George Sand. I couldn't read them. I've always had some kind of instinctive idea of what constitutes what I want to read as opposed to great literature. I didn't read the Russian novelists till I was in my thirties. And I didn't read Flaubert until I was in my late thirties. And if you can write a novel like they wrote—hey, I'm waiting till I'm old enough; I'm too young for that now. You have to know a lot to write that way. My great-grandfather, the Lebanese one, was a poet; he used to publish his poetry. And it was in Arabic.

And those chants—I don't know if you've ever heard them —but at family gatherings one of my uncles would chant them in classic Arabic, not village Lebanese. The classic Arabic he sang was beautiful. It just transports you to some other kind of realm and it's very similar to what happens at one of the dances. The sensation is the same. You move out of the narrow-minded sphere of day-to-day life into a transcendent space. And that's art. I'm sure that that's art. And I'm sure that that's everywhere on earth. Every people has some way of forming a language that moves you, that moves you beyond. It doesn't just move you; it moves you some place else. And it doesn't much matter to me where they come from, if I can understand and it has that influence on me, then I take it as a model.

LC   Can you speak a little bit more about your works in progress?

ALLEN Ah, well, let's see. Mention my novel. This novel's fun. I'm calling it a medicine-dyke novel. It's partly a joke. I just want to see if I can write a popular novel because I think everyone should be able to do that. And it's partly very serious. Because there are certain understandings of how ritual works, and I want to be in the popular mind that accurate. It's a novel about the nuclear stuff—about bombs, but it's not about "Oh look, they're going to kill us." It's about "Look, the grandmother is coming." It's a novel about old Indian women and young Indian women. It's about alcoholism and battery. What I'm trying to do is pose two communities, an Indian community and a lesbian community, with characters that bridge both communities. So, of course, it's really a bridge novel. And I'm bridging different kinds of realities as well as different communities. It's complex. I laugh and say, "It's my *War and Peace*," because it's going to take at least a thousand pages to do what I want. So probably I'm going to write it as a trilogy, because I don't want to sacrifice any of the stories. I could, but I don't want to. There's a family—there's a lesbian in the family, a young woman, and then her mother, Margaret, who's single, and there's Margaret's son, who's an alcoholic, and his girlfriend-wife. So there's that whole family complex. And then the young woman who's a lesbian is connected to the mother's best friend, who's also a lesbian, but who's an Indian. There's all these interconnections and I'm having a grand time writing it—it's really fun. I'm going to be reading from it tomorrow night. And I read from it, maybe a month ago; the reception was very good. People like it. It's funny, it's delightful; it's a little scary. It's very serious. And it's a romp. It's an adventure story. So that's one.

The Beacon [Press] book—collection of literary and feminist essays put together—*The Sacred Hoop: Recovering the Feminine in American Indian Literature.* I keep wondering if the world's ready for a feminist Indian book, but there it is. Then, oh, the Lebanese people. I've been working on this one for twelve years. And it's hard. But I've been doing research on Lebanon, on the contemporary situation in Lebanon. My father's family are Maronites. And, you know, we're the bad guys now. And I equate that in my mind to when my uncle, my Indian uncle, used to ride the train. But when he got on the train he would say that he was Italian because he didn't want to say that he's Indian because he knew that would be a bad thing to do. People would spit on him. So he'd say he was Italian. That was fine. And I think that being a Maronite now is similar to being an Indian fifty or a hundred years ago in the United States. And I'm trying to find out in my research if what I said is true. I think that the Maronite people are facing extermination. I think that they're facing genocide. And I think that in 1985 they're in the same position that the Plains Indians were in 1885. That's how I'm approaching it. But while I'm at it, I'm also looking at the old, old, ancient layers of civilization there, and I'm finding all this goddess stuff, all this woman culture—Ishtar and Isis and so forth. So I'm having a grand time with that book. I guess that's all.

I've begun a new poetry manuscript; not *Skins and Bones* —that's done. But it's called "Soundings." You know how you make soundings in the depth? There are some experimental language poetry poems, but I'm trying to work with traditional Anglo-European forms, with heavy rhyme and deep allusion and intense metaphor, obscure references. And to speak of how you discover the depth of what's so, of what's true, of what resounds clearly and what's murky. And I guess you can say it's my way of finding out who I am, but not really. It's really a record of how you go from adulthood to old age. That is to say, that middle passage, because that's where I am now. And I'm very preoccupied with it. I've been writing some articles on menopause, and I'm interested in the change of consciousness that goes on. My own experience is that my mind is changing dramatically as I move toward fifty. And I imagine fifty as some sort of a gate; the door is going to open and I'm going to be somebody else. And it's like a ten-, twelve-year passage. It's a very long one. And that's what the book is exploring. But it's barely begun it.

Louise Erdrich and Michael Dorris

Louise Erdrich was born in 1954 in Little Falls, North Dakota, and she attended schools at Wahpeton. Her father is of German descent and her mother is a Turtle Mountain Chippewa. After graduating from Dartmouth in 1976 with a major in English and creative writing, Erdrich returned to North Dakota, where she conducted poetry workshops throughout the state under the auspices of the Poetry in the Schools Program of the North Dakota Arts Council. She later entered the creative-writing program at Johns Hopkins University, directed by Richard Howard. After receiving a master's degree in creative writing, she moved to Boston, where she became editor of the Boston Indian Council newspaper, The Circle.

Michael Dorris arrived at Dartmouth College in 1972 to join and later to direct the Native American Studies Program. Erdrich and Dorris met at Dartmouth and were married in 1981.

First a poet and then a novelist (her collected poems, Jacklight, *were published in 1984), Erdrich's short stories have appeared in many important magazines. Working with Michael Dorris, she turned the stories published between 1982 and 1984 into a novel,* Love Medicine *(1984), which received enthusiastic praise. Among its many awards, the novel was named the best work of fiction of 1984 by the National Book Critics Circle.*

Michael Dorris was born in 1945 and grew up in Washington, Idaho, Kentucky, and Montana. A member of the Modoc tribe on his father's side, he received a bachelor's degree in English and classics from Georgetown University in 1967 and a master's in philosophy from Yale University in 1971. He has recently left Dartmouth College, where he was professor of anthropology and Native American studies, to devote himself to writing.

His many scholarly publications include A Guide to Research on North American Indians *(1983), with Arlene Hirschfelder and Mary Lou Byler, and* Native Americans: Five Hundred Years After *(1977).*

The unique collaboration between Louise Erdrich and Michael Dorris is explained by Michael himself: "We go over every word and achieve consensus on every word; basically we agree on every word when it's finally finished." They are currently writing together a four-volume family saga, three volumes of which have been published under Erdrich's name: Love Medicine *(1984),* The Beet Queen *(1986), and* Tracks *(1988). In addition, they have collaborated on* A Yellow Raft in Blue Water *(1987), a novel, and* The Broken Cord, *a book on fetal alcohol syndrome in Indian reservations. Both of these are under Dorris's name.*

Erdrich and Dorris live in Cornish, New Hampshire, with their family. They are the parents of six children: three children adopted by Dorris as a single parent whom Erdrich has since adopted and three children born since their marriage.

On September 17, 1985, I met with the Dorris family at Northfield, Minnesota, where Michael was spending a sabbatical. Incessant, simultaneous activities were going on in their house: Dorris, who acts as the couple's literary agent, was constantly interrupted by the telephone; Louise was busy with the youngest child, Pallas; Madeline, eleven, kept trying to find peace from her three-year-old sister, Persia; the computer printer was noisily doing its job somewhere. The creative process seemed to be perfectly shared.

LC What's the source of your storytelling technique?

DORRIS Louise had two stories that were independent stories, "Scales" and "The Red Convertible." They were published independently and then there was a contest for the Nelson Algren Award for which they solicited stories of some five thousand or so words. We got the announcement that it was due by the fifteenth of January, and this was the first of January, and we just got back from vacation, and so we started talking about it and out of that grew "The World's Greatest Fishermen," the opening story of the novel *Love Medicine*, and we sent it off and thought of all the things that were wrong with it and what we would revise when it came back, and lo and behold, it won that contest. There were thousands of entries. We said, if it's that good maybe we ought to think about expanding this and telling that same story, because there are many stories in that story, from other points of view. And that expanded to developing the characters of Nector and Marie and Lulu and on and on. At first it was, I think, a series of stories, many of which were published independently, and then in the last several drafts we went back and tied them together. We realized some of the people who had different names were in fact the same character and that they would unite, very much the same way that this book has now turned into four books, because the next book, which is titled *The Beet Queen*, takes place in a small town just off the reservation where *Love Medicine* takes place. And some of the characters, Eli, for instance, are in that, and one of the main characters in *The Beet Queen* is Dot Adare, who married Gerry Nanapush in that book, and we didn't realize who it was until it was almost done. And then *Tracks*, which is the third book, takes the older character in both *Love Medicine* and *The Beet Queen* back a generation into a traditional time; and the fourth book, to be titled *American Horse*, will take the younger characters forward for a few years. It's a saga that takes place over about eighty years, a hundred years, and is an analogy in a way, of all the processes that people in this part of the country have gone through.

The Turtle Mountain Chippewa people are an interesting group because they came originally from northern Minnesota but are heavily mixed with French and Cree, and so the language that they speak up there is called Michif, which is a combination of all those. And for instance, Lipsha, the character in *Love Medicine*, is Michif bastardization for *le petit chou*, the French expression of endearment, "my little cabbage," and that's where the name comes from. The traditional music in Turtle Mountain is fiddle music and there are a lot of French names up there.

LC   So is it a kind of traditional tribal storytelling technique?

DORRIS   It's cyclical in that respect and that's why it's disturbing that the last line of the Italian translation does not bring her back into it,[1] because basically this is the story of the reverberation of June's life even though she is the one character who does not have her own voice. Bringing her home is finally in fact resolving her life and death in balance.

LC   Can you speak about the point of view in *Love Medicine*?

DORRIS   It's what Louise does best, basically. Every one of these stories went through seven, eight drafts, some in third person, some in the voice of a different character, and basically the voices that emerge are the ones that work best. One of my roles in this was to tell Louise that she really did it well. We all think we should be able to do that thing which was hardest for us rather than things which are easiest for us. First-person narrative is easiest for Louise; she does it best. It's not easy, but she does it best. It is a story cycle in the traditional sense. One of the interesting reviews of the book was talking about the fact that nobody in the book is right, that in fact it is community voice, that the point of view is the community voice and the means of exchanging information is gossip, and so consequently there is no narrator; there is no single protagonist, but rather it is the entire community dealing with the upheavals that emerge from the book and now will emerge from four books. [Louise returns from feeding the baby.] Now you can speak for yourself.

LC   In *Love Medicine*, one character, Lipsha, was happy because he hadn't yet acquired a memory, and Granpa was happy because he was losing his. Memory then is a burden instead of being a source to shape a new identity and as a link between past and present.

ERDRICH   That's an interesting tie. I guess for Nector the events of his life and his guilt made his memory a burden for him. It's certainly not a burden for everyone in the book. But for him I think the guilt of his association with his mistress, with Lulu, his rejection of her and burning her house down, whether he causes it directly or not, made memory something he is not happy to live with.

LC   The multiethnic family is at the center of *Love Medicine*. How do you see the future generations of American Indians from this perspective?

DORRIS   The only multiethnic person, really, is King's wife, Lynette. Marie is a mixed-blood herself.

ERDRICH   Well, everybody has a lot of French, but in particular the French and the Indian had been so blended by that time, it's a new culture. I don't know what to think about it; I haven't really thought a lot about what the future would be. I suppose more of the same. [To Michael.] What do you think? Have you thought about that?

DORRIS   Well, I think one question people ask us and have been asking since 1620 is "Are Indians vanishing?" "Are Indians going away?" I think the answer to that question would be no. Maybe native tribal culture has changed like all cultures, and *Love Medicine* is a story about a contemporary group of people that are in some ways indistinguishable from other rural North Dakota people who are not rich, but in other ways they are very much unique, very much who they were; they have the same kind of symbols that inspired Chippewas in the past, the water and the water god, and they have the kind of family connection which has always been the core of the tribe, I think. It is more subtle than when people dressed differently and when people spoke different languages and everything but not less real.

LC   Your poems in *Jacklight* show a remarkable narrative power and a tense poetic language. What's the impact of the storyteller upon the poet?

ERDRICH   Probably it's more the other way around. I began as a poet, writing poetry, I began to tell stories in the poems and then realized that there was not enough room in a poem unless you are a John Milton and write enormous volumes of poetry. There was not enough room to really tell the story. I just began to realize that I wanted to be a fiction writer; that's a bigger medium, you know. I have a lot more room and it's closer to the oral tradition of sitting around and telling stories. But I think in the book you try to make the language do some of the same things, metaphorically and sensuously, physically, that poetry can do. So the poems had a real effect on the storytelling. But when I wrote the poetry I never had tried writing fiction before, so it was prior to all of the other stories.

LC   But do you consider yourself a poet or a storyteller?

ERDRICH   Oh, a storyteller, a writer.

LC   Humor is one of the most important features of contemporary
              Native American literature. Is there a difference in the use of
              humor in the old Indian stories and in the contemporary ones?

ERDRICH   The humor is a little blacker and bleaker now.

DORRIS   Louise, have you talked about the ways in which we sort of
              consciously saw this book differently from much other contem-
              porary fiction by American Indians? Most of the others, I am
              sure Laura is aware of, deal with contact in one way or another
              —what is the impact of leaving the reservation, coming back
              to the reservation—but the outside world very much imposes
              on the characters. In some of the drafts of *Love Medicine* that
              was the case, the characters went to Washington, or one thing or
              another, and basically we made a conscious decision, in the way
              Louise wrote the book, to have it all centered in a community
              in which the outside world is not very present or very relevant
              in some respects. This is a world that is encompassed by that
              community, and it isn't so much the outside world of discrimi-
              nation or wealth or anything like that, but rather this is how a
              community deals with itself and with the members of itself.

ERDRICH   To go back just for one second, I really think the question about
              humor is very important. It's one of the most important parts of
              American Indian life and literature, and one thing that always
              hits us is just that Indian people really have a great sense of hu-
              mor and when it's survival humor, you learn to laugh at things.
              It's really there, and I think Simon Ortiz is one person who has
              a lot of funny things happen, but a lot of terrible things as well
              in his work. It's just a personal way of responding to the world
              and to things that happen to you; it's a different way of looking
              at the world, very different from the stereotype, the stoic, un-
              flinching Indian standing, looking at the sunset. It's really there,
              the humor, and I really hope that beside the serious parts in this
              particular book, people would see the humor.

LC   Do you see, then, American Indian literature as a multiethnic
              literature?

ERDRICH   One of the big mistakes that a lot of people make in coming
              to American Indian literature is thinking, oh, if it's Indian it's
              Indian. It's just like being in Europe and saying French literature
              is European literature. Well, of course, French, Italian, German,
              any culture, has its own literature, its own background, its own

language, that springs from that culture. The thing that we have in common is that English is a language which has been imposed on Indian people through a whole series of concerted efforts. Almost all American Indian writers speak English as their main language, as their first language, but they all come out of a different heritage, background, a different worldview, a different mythology.

LC   Do American Indian writers have a large audience among Indian people? Do Indian people see the writer's work as a means to preserve their culture?

ERDRICH   My first audience that I would write for, that we write for, as a couple, is American Indians, hoping that they will read, laugh, cry, really take in the work. One of the problems is the distribution of literature. For instance, how many Indians can afford to buy *Love Medicine* right now? It's pretty expensive and it's the way publishing unfortunately goes on. One of our hopes was to have it available in a nice, cheap edition everywhere, so that people could get it easily.

LC   Does literature develop a sense of Pan-Indianness?

ERDRICH   Oh, yes, I think it does. There is a whole rich mine of Pan-Indian culture people circulate, and I am sure literature is certainly one of those things. Michael has had lots of mail from readers of *Love Medicine*, Indians from different tribes who have read it and said, "This is what happened here and it's so much like what happened to me, or to someone I know." It's a kind of universalizing experience. The book does touch some universals, which is what we're talking about, Pan-Indianism. We wanted the reservation in *Love Medicine* to kind of ring true to people from lots of different tribes.

LC   American Indian literature in mainstream American literature. What's its place and its contribution?

ERDRICH   I don't distinguish the two. I don't think American Indian literature should be distinguished from mainstream literature. Setting it apart and saying that people with special interest might read this literature sets Indians apart too.

LC   I am not distinguishing, I am not setting American Indian literature apart from mainstream literature. Still, in American literature you have black, Jewish, Chicano literature, and so on.

ERDRICH   I was thinking ours contributes to literature as a whole in a

47

way that any book would. You have a view into someone's life that you could not have had without this particular book and its vision. It's contributing in that way. I think that Jean Rhys said something about her contribution being a small tributary to the great lake of literature. I think that's the same way any writer feels. To contribute to the great run of literature is very worthy.

LC   Can you speak about the contribution in terms of themes and style?

ERDRICH   Writing is different from tribe to tribe, the images are different from tribe to tribe.

LC   What do you think of non-Indian critics and readers of your work and of American Indian literature in general?

ERDRICH   I never expected to get a letter back about this book, and there have been letters you would not believe; people just baring their souls. I think they really felt some kind of kinship with people in the book. People who are not Indians are writing these letters, too; it doesn't matter to me, I am glad for readers, as any writer is, I think, so I feel grateful. I want to be able to present Indian people as sympathetic characters, nonstereotypes, characters that any non-Indian would identify with. If they read the book with a certain kind of sympathy, I'm glad. What can I do but to be grateful for non-Indian critics who bring the work into a greater circulation and interest other people in it.

LC   What about the European approach toward American Indian literature?

ERDRICH   I suppose I don't really know. I know that Karl May had a great effect on the German imagination. Anyway I think more interest is there, because so much of what is being written now is breaking the stereotypes and giving a different view of American Indians than Karl May could have. Because of his writing there's this fertile kind of ground, a thirst for American Indian literature, but goodness, there is more than Karl May. There are people writing who really write out of the tradition, who really are fascinating writers. There is that romanticizing aspect too, at least I am familiar with some Germans' attitude toward American Indian literature, but I think the distance between American Indians and Europeans is another factor, because people who live near Indians have the worst kind of prejudice—people who are competing for the same land. Probably there is less prejudice in Europe toward American Indians. I think that's how Indians feel in general; there is just less prejudice.

LC   Has there been any one major influence on your writing?

ERDRICH Michael, of course. He has been a major influence. He really is. I am indebted to him for organizing and making the book into a novel. I tended to be a person who thought in terms of stories and poems and short things. The book became a novel because of Michael. He came one day and said pretty much, "Oh, this is a novel," and you know, we began to write it in that way. So it's Michael. I would probably be a poet or a short-story writer, not a novelist. And other writers have influenced me. Certainly Toni Morrison, Barbara Pym, the English novelists.

LC   You mentioned Faulkner before.

ERDRICH [William] Faulkner, [Italo] Calvino. For me Calvino is one of the most wonderful writers, and the magic in his work is something that has been an influence, as well as the South American, Latin American, writers.

LC   Are you going to write a screenplay from *Love Medicine*?

DORRIS It may be; it's not clear. I am doing a book, two books, this year myself, with my name on them, but we are doing them together, in the same way. One is a nonfiction book on fetal alcohol syndrome on reservations, and another is a novel which is about people on a reservation farther west than this. *The Broken Cord* is about what happens when on some reservations a very large percentage of children are born with birth defects that come from their mothers' drinking during pregnancy. They are very subtle birth defects, sometimes that you can't see, but they paralyze the ability to think abstractedly and they complicate long-term choices. And how these communities cope with that. I was at a reservation last week doing some interviews for that.

LC   How large is the percentage and where is this syndrome most widespread?

DORRIS Fetal alcohol syndrome is a condition that exists, mostly undiagnosed, in all parts of the world where women consume alcohol during their pregnancies. Countries in which it is reported to be most serious include the Soviet Union, France, Sweden, the United States, and Japan. In some communities in this country, including some American Indian reservations, it is estimated that if current trends continue something in excess of 50 percent of all babies born in the year 2000 A.D. will be impaired to some degree by FAS or FAE [fetal alcohol effect]. The only truly safe policy is no drinking at all during pregnancy or breast-feeding, since alcohol affects different women in various ways.

LC Could you describe your writing process?

ERDRICH Now we don't know what to do because we don't have a big table in the living room. Back in New Hampshire, we put the table out, and we could work with the whole manuscript at the end, when it was about finished. But Michael will have a draft and show me and we will talk it over, or I'll have a draft, talk about the whole plan of it, characters out of it, just talk over every aspect of it.

DORRIS We get to know the characters very well and talk about them and every situation. If we are in a restaurant, we imagine what so-and-so would order from the menu, and what so-and-so would choose from this catalog, so that we get to know them in a full way, and when they appear on the page, they have that fullness behind them even though it doesn't all get written about.

LC But who actually writes down the page?

DORRIS Louise. In *Love Medicine.*

ERDRICH Michael writes down on his page, or I write down on my page. I go and work in my room, and in *A Yellow Raft in Blue Water*, Michael goes and works on his computer. He can write right on the screen, right on the keyboard.

DORRIS And we edit it together. We go over every word and achieve consensus on every word; basically we agree on every word when it's finally finished.

LC Did it work that way for *Love Medicine* too?

DORRIS Yes.

ERDRICH Yes, we go through——

DORRIS Every sentence!

ERDRICH Any!

DORRIS Many times, many times. Two times at the very end when it's all finished, then we sit down with the entire manuscript and talk about the manuscript and read it aloud at each other. We just did this with *The Beet Queen*, and it took about four weeks

	to go through what we thought was the finished manuscript, and in the course of that we cut thirty pages because it was like pinching it and squeezing it and thirty pages fell out.
LC	Could you speak a little bit more about your works in progress?
ERDRICH	Michael's work is what we're working on now. He's writing a novel [*A Yellow Raft in Blue Water*] that has to do with a young teen-age girl who has a series of comic and tragic and explosive experiments. She gets into situations. One of my favorites is when she takes over for one of her cousins who is incapacitated, who can't ride his horse in a rodeo, and she rides the horse.
DORRIS	She is a combination ethnically; her father is black and her mother is Indian, and so there is another multiethnic combination.
ERDRICH	It hasn't been written very much at all, it's really fascinating.
DORRIS	Not so uncommon. It's very common in certain parts of the country. *Tracks*, the third book in the *Love Medicine* quartet takes place from 1915 to 1927 and acts as a kind of "pre-quel" to *Love Medicine* and *The Beet Queen*. It is narrated by an elderly man, Nanapush, and a young girl, Pauline. Parts of it have or will appear in *Esquire* [August 1986, "Fleur," which went on to win the National Magazine Award for fiction and the O. Henry first prize], *Harper's* [May 1987, "Scales"], and the *Atlantic* [March 1988, "Matchimanito"]. *Tracks* will be published by Henry Holt in September 1988, and in paperback by Harper and Row a year later. The fourth and last book of the quartet, "American Horse," is under way and should be published in a couple of years. It will begin in 1972 and go to the present. My next novel, "The Cloud Chamber," is also under way, as well as a new collection of poems by Louise and a coauthored novel by both of us. *Tracks* was the first one to have the finished draft, but it will be the third one to be published, and it's going to be thoroughly revised and changed in the light of the characters that we know from the other books.
LC	By Louise Erdrich or by Michael Dorris?
DORRIS	By Louise.
LC	I understand that your names are interchangeable.
DORRIS	In some ways, yes. We actually write some stories for popular consumption under the pen name of Milou North, and they

have been published a lot in England and also in this country. So actually we write some less serious things together.

LC   Considering that you write as a couple, is there any significant change in *Yellow Raft* with respect to *Love Medicine* and *The Beet Queen*?

DORRIS   The answer is yes. It's about different characters, and therefore the voices are different, as is the setting. While we labor closely with each other in all phases of making a book, Louise and I each have our own relationships with the particular work.

LC   Can you see any evolution in your work?

ERDRICH   It's the hardest thing for a writer to get a grasp on. I mean, you almost have to be removed to see.

DORRIS   I think more confidence, maybe, and a greater risk-taking.

ERDRICH   It's true. The forms of the work are loosening up.

DORRIS   We have written so many pages between the two of us, only a very small tip of the iceberg actually sees print.

Joy Harjo

Joy Harjo was born in Tulsa, Oklahoma, in 1951. She is a member of the Creek tribe. She attended high school at the Institute of American Indian Arts in Santa Fe and received a B.A. degree from the University of New Mexico and an M.F.A. degree from the University of Iowa's Writers' Workshop. A filmmaker, artist, and television scriptwriter, she is recognized as one of the most gifted poets of her generation. She has taught Native American literature and creative writing at the Institute of American Indian Arts, Arizona State University, and the University of Colorado, Boulder. She has two children and currently lives in Tucson, where she teaches at the University of Arizona.

Very active in community service, she is on the board of directors for the National Association for Third World Writers, on the policy panel of the National Endowment for the Arts, and a member of the board of directors for the Native American Public Broadcasting Consortium. She is also contributing editor of Contact II, *the poetry editor of* High Plains Literary Review, *and contributing editor for* Tyuonyi. *She has traveled extensively through the United States, conducting workshops and giving poetry readings. Her publications include two highly praised collections of poems,* She Had Some Horses *(1983) and* In Mad Love and War *(1990), and* Secrets from the Center of the World *(1989), a book of prose poems with photographs by Stephen Strom.*

Reflecting on her responsibility as a writer, she says: "I feel strongly that I have a responsibility to all the sources that I am: to all past and future ancestors, to my home country, to all places that I touch down on and that are myself, to all voices, all women, all of my tribe, all people, all earth, and beyond that to all beginnings and endings. In a strange kind of sense it frees me to believe in myself, to be able to speak, to have voice, because I have to; it is my survival." [1]

We met on September 23, 1985, at her home in Denver. Strikingly old and young at the same time, her being "memory alive" —memory like "a delta in the skin"—comes out from every word she says, from recent or distant years, from the quiet yet poignant intensity of her voice as she reads her new poems.

LC   When did you start writing?

HARJO   Not until I was about twenty-two, which I've always thought fairly late. Up to that time I was mostly interested in art, especially painting, and majored in it at the University of New Mexico until my last year, when I transferred to the English Department to graduate with a creative-writing major. I went on to get my M.F.A. in creative writing from the University of Iowa.

LC   Why did you shift from being an art major to creative writing?

HARJO   Because I found that language, through poetry, was taking on more magical qualities than my painting. I could say more when I wrote. Soon it wasn't a choice. Poetry-speaking "called me" in a sense. And I couldn't say no.

LC   Could you speak about going back to your roots, in your poetry, of your Oklahoma land and heritage?

HARJO   I just finished a poem today. It's about trying to find the way back. But it's a different place, a mythical place. It's a spiritual landscape that Oklahoma is a part of—I always see Oklahoma as my mother, my motherland. I am connected psychically; there is a birth cord that connects me. But I don't live there and don't know that I ever will. It's too familiar, and too painful. My son lives there now; he's going to Sequoyah High School, a tribal school that is now managed by the Cherokee tribe.

So my return usually takes place on a mythical level. I mean, I do travel there as often as I can. I've written a literary column for my tribal newspaper, the *Muscogee Nation News*, know my relatives, keep in touch. There are many memories there for me, it's one of my homes.

LC How much does your Creek heritage affect your work as a poet?

HARJO It provides the underlying psychic structure, within which is a wealth of memory. I was not brought up traditionally Creek, was raised in the north side of Tulsa in a neighborhood where there lived many other mixed-blood Indian families. My neighbors were Seminole Indian, Pawnee, other tribes, and white. I know when I write there is an old Creek within me that often participates.

LC You said once, memory is like "a delta in the skin," so you are "memory alive," your poetry stems from memory always at work.[2]

HARJO It is Creek, and touches in on the larger tribal continental memory and the larger human memory, global. It's not something I consciously chose; I mean, I am not a full-blood, but it was something that chose me, that lives in me, and I cannot deny it. Sometimes I wish I could disappear into the crowds of the city and lose this responsibility, because it is a responsibility. But I can't. I also see memory as not just associated with past history, past events, past stories, but nonlinear, as in future and ongoing history, events, and stories. And it changes.

LC You see a very close relationship between writing poetry and "digging piles of earth with a stick: smell it, form it."[3] So, does it mean you're still looking for your roots down there?

HARJO They're there. That's no question. When I speak of roots I often mean more than what's usually conjectured. I consider the place we all came from, since the very beginning. It's a place I don't yet have a language for. But, on the more mundane level, I did drive around the United States in my car, alone, about three or four summers ago—just to know it better, this beautiful land. And one place that was most important for me to visit was outside a little town in Alabama called Atmore. There is still a settlement of Creeks there, who hung on through the destruction set off by Andrew Jackson's greed. I went there to say hello, and they welcomed me, treated me well. There is a communication beginning between the Oklahoma Creeks and the Alabama Creeks. We [Oklahoma Creeks] still have the language, the dances, ceremonies, which they have lost much of, but then again, nothing has destroyed their memory, which is strong, and which has kept their small enclave alive through these years of the racist South. I was so proud of them, am proud that they have kept their Creekness alive when Jackson meant them to be destroyed.

My family on my father's side was originally from Alabama. They were forced to leave during the time of Removal [1832], which really wasn't that long ago. In fact, my great-great-grand-father, Menawha, led the Redstick War of the Creeks against Andrew Jackson. Of course, we know what happened, and Mena-wha and his family were forced into Oklahoma. Menawha said he never wanted to see a white face again; from that part of my family we were rebels, and speakers. So what I am doing makes sense in terms of a family memory.

LC   Do you look at writing as a means of survival?

HARJO   Sure. I have to. On both a personal level and a larger, communal level. I don't believe I would be alive today if it hadn't been for writing. There were times when I was conscious of holding onto a pen and letting the words flow, painful and from the gut, to keep from letting go of it all. Now, this was when I was much younger, and full of self-hatred. Writing helped me give voice to turn around a terrible silence that was killing me. And on a larger level, if we, as Indian people, Indian women, keep silent, then we will disappear, at least in this level of reality. As Audre Lorde says, also, "Your silence will not protect you," which has been a quietly unanimous decision it seems, this last century with Indian people.[4]

LC   *She Had Some Horses* is a kind of circular journey, walking and talking backward. "Call it Fear" is the very first poem and in the last one, "I Give You Back," "the terrible and beautiful fear" comes to an end. Could you elaborate on that?

HARJO   "Call it Fear" was one of the earliest poems I wrote in that series, and "I Give You Back" one of the last. I didn't consciously set up the structure of the book that way, but maybe unconsciously I did. I want to thank Brenda Petersen, a novelist-editor friend of mine, for her arrangement. I gave her the manuscript when I couldn't get the arrangement right after many, many tries, and it

Joy Harjo

<table>
<tr><td></td><td>is because of her that it works well. She understood that I meant a circular journey.</td></tr>
<tr><td>LC</td><td>In the last section of the same book you see in the horses the coming of a new people. Does it also shape your identity as a woman?</td></tr>
<tr><td>HARJO</td><td>I'm not sure I know what you mean. When I consider a new people, I consider a people whose spiritual selves are obvious. There are no judgments, or prejudices. Sexual identities are not cause for power plays, and we become fully who we are, whether male, female, or any combination. We need this resurrection; it's who we truly are, yet you could be deceived, especially when you look around the world and see the hatred against the female, and notice, too, that all the wars are basically race wars, white people against the darker-skinned ones. But I am especially speaking of a power that would be called women-woman-intuitive. My work is woman-identified. One of the funniest questions I've been asked as a visitor to an Indian-culture class in a university is, by a male student, "Where are the men in your poems?" He was offended because he didn't see himself, not in the form that he looked for. I truly feel there is a new language coming about —look at the work of Meridel LeSueur, Sharon Doubiago, Linda Hogan, Alice Walker—it's coming from the women. Something has to be turned around.</td></tr>
<tr><td>LC</td><td>The moon image is central to your poetry. Moon as wholeness, which speaks of the universe, a circular design again, which speaks also of woman's life. Is that true?</td></tr>
<tr><td>HARJO</td><td>Yes, although she appears less and less in my new poems. I associate the moon with the past, evoking the past, past fears, and so on.</td></tr>
<tr><td>LC</td><td>Your personal past?</td></tr>
<tr><td>HARJO</td><td>Anyone's personal past. Now I am looking toward fire, a renewal. But still aware of the dream, in which the moon appears, a constructive kind of dreaming.</td></tr>
<tr><td>LC</td><td>What do you mean by constructive?</td></tr>
<tr><td>HARJO</td><td>I mean, consciously understanding that dreamtime is another kind of cohesive reality that we take part in.</td></tr>
<tr><td>LC</td><td>A kind of active perception instead of a passive one.</td></tr>
<tr><td>HARJO</td><td>Yes, it's much more active.</td></tr>
</table>

LC	Feminism and tribal heritage—can you see any connection?
HARJO	The world has changed so much. Yes, I'm sure there is a connection, but so much differs from tribe to tribe.
LC	Because some Indian cultures are woman-oriented?
HARJO	Some are woman-oriented, especially when you consider the earth as woman, like the Pueblo people of the Southwest. But all have changed over the years after much white contact. And values have changed. Many have evolved, or devolved, into male-centered, male-dominated cultures, following the pattern of the dominant Euro-culture that is American, but generally women were, are, recognized as physically, electrically, whatever, more grounded, in tune with the earth, and again, that's a generalization, because there are always exceptions. You will find "grounded" men, also. I still don't feel as if I have answered your question. I know I walk in and out of several worlds everyday. Some overlap, some never will, or at least not as harmoniously. The word "feminism" doesn't carry over to the tribal world, but a concept mirroring similar meanings would. Let's see, what would it then be called—empowerment, some kind of empowerment.
LC	What does it mean, being an American Indian woman in the United States nowadays?
HARJO	To begin, it certainly means you are a survivor. Indian people make up only about one-half of 1 percent of the total population of the United States! It means you carry with you a certain unique perception. And again you are dealing with tribal differences, personal differences, and so on. We are not all alike! Yet, I believe there is a common dream, a common thread between us, mostly unspoken.

I don't believe there are any accidents in why people were born where they were, who they were, or are. There are no accidents. So I realize that being born an American Indian woman in this time and place is with a certain reason, a certain purpose. There are seeds of dreams I hold, and responsibility, that go with being born someone, especially a woman of my tribe, who is also part of this invading other culture, and the larger globe. We in this generation, and the next generation, are dealing with a larger world than the people who went before us— |

that we know of, because who knows what went down many, many, many years ago that no one remembers. We are dealing with a world consciousness, and have begun to see unity, first with many tribes in the United States and North America with the Pan-Indian movement, and now with tribal people in the rest of the world, Central and South America, Africa, Australian aborigines, and so on. We are not isolated. No one is. What happens here, happens there. But it is on sometimes subtle yet disturbing levels.

LC   Are you active in women's organizations?

HARJO   Not really. Sometimes I feel I should be, but it isn't my manner. I participate by doing benefit readings, appearances, taking part when it is useful to do so. I know it is important, and groups are more powerful than one person working alone, but I guess there is no one group that I feel strong enough about to be active in, though I actively take part in many.

LC   Are you suspicious? Of what?

HARJO   I've wondered. Maybe it comes from being a mixed-blood in this world. I mean, I feel connected to others, but many women's groups have a majority of white women and I honestly can feel uncomfortable, or even voiceless sometimes. I've lived in and out of both worlds for a long time and have learned how to speak —those groups just affect others that way—with a voicelessness. It's my problem, something I've learned to get over, am learning to overcome, because I am often the only one to speak for many of us in those situations. Sometimes it gets pretty comical, bizarre. When I was on the National Endowment for the Arts literature panel I was often the spokesperson-representative for Indian people, black people, all minority people, including women's, lesbian, and gay groups. It was rather ridiculous and angering at the same time, for we were all considered outside the mainstream of American literature. And it's not true, for often we are closer to the center.

LC   Noni Daylight appears in some of your poems, persona poems. You said, "It's like she was a good friend."[5] Would you comment on that, on the persona in your poems?

HARJO   She began quite some time ago, as a name I gave a real-life woman I couldn't name in a poem. Then she evolved into her own person, took on her own life. And then she left my poems and went into a poem by Barney Bush, a Shawnee poet, and I never saw her again. She never came back!

LC   What about the other stories of women in your poems? Are they true stories?

HARJO Yes, always on some level. I'm a writer, I like to make up stories, to add to them, often make them larger. The "I" is not always me, but a way I chose to speak the poem. "The Woman Hanging from the Thirteenth Floor" is written around an imaginary woman. You could call her imaginary. But within that space she is real, also. I made a trip to Chicago, oh, about eight years ago, and one of the places I went to while I was there was the Chicago Indian Center. The center was rather bleak, as there wasn't extra money around to buy things to make the place warm, home-like; there were no curtains, nothing like that, but in one room I noticed a rocking chair. It may have been empty, or there may have been someone in it—the image stayed with me. Perhaps it was because the chair was round, and everything else, all around, was square. So, a few years after that trip, the image stayed with me, and I would see this woman, rocking and rocking, for her life, and she compelled me to write the poem. And I felt her standing behind me, urging me on as I wrote, kept looking behind me. When it first appeared, and during the first readings of the poem others would come up after the reading and say, "You know, I know that woman," or "I knew her," or "I heard the story and have a newspaper clipping of it," and the event always had occurred in a different place. And other women are composites of many women I know, or stories I've heard, probably much like a fiction writer would work.

LC   So you became a kind of storyteller?

HARJO In a way, though I am not a good fiction writer, or should I say, have never really tried it, except in terms of screenplays.

LC   "Language identifies the world." You said that the English language is not enough. "It is a male language, not tribal, not spiritual enough."[6]

HARJO Yes, I said that. I have learned to love the language, or rather, what the language can express. But I have felt bound by the strictness imposed by its male-centeredness, its emphasis on nouns. So, it's also challenging, as a poet, to use it to express tribal, spiritual language, being. But maybe all poets basically are after that, and sometimes it isn't enough and that's when those boundaries become frustrating.

LC   What do you mean by saying English is not enough, English is a male language?

HARJO Again, maybe it would be that way in any language, the sense of somehow being at a loss for words; [that] could always be the poet's dilemma. The ending of a poem, "Bleed-Through," says it: "There are no words, only sounds / that lead us into the darkest nights / where stars burn into ice / where the dead arise again / to walk in shoes of fire."

LC   Since language has an importance of its own in Indian culture, what's the contribution or influence, just in terms of language, to mainstream American literature?

HARJO What I think of immediately is the denial, the incredible denial of anything other than that based on the European soul in American literature. Anything else is seen as "foreign," or not consciously integrated into what is called American literature. It could be ethnocentrism backed by a terrible guilt about what happened in this country.

LC   So what's the contribution, just in terms of language, to mainstream American literature?

HARJO That's a difficult question, one that will take me many months to consider, because I'm always thinking about what I can add to the language, as someone of this background—dreams, and so on. I consider first a certain lyricism, a land-based language.

LC   The spirit of place?

HARJO Yes, the spirit of place recognized, fed, not even paved over, forgotten. Sometimes I feel like specters of forgotten ones roam the literature of some of these American writers who don't understand where they come from, who they are, where they are going. The strongest writers have always been the ones with a well-defined sense of place—I don't mean you have to be a nature writer—I'm thinking of "nonethnic" people, like Flannery O'Connor.

LC   What about imagery?

HARJO Oh sure, imagery. That's definitely part of it.

63

LC   A new feeling of landscape perhaps?

HARJO   Or a knowing of the landscape, as something alive with personality, breathing. Alive with names, alive with events, nonlinear. It's not static and that's a very important point. The Western viewpoint has always been one of the land as wilderness, something to be afraid of, and conquered because of the fear.

LC   The so-called wilderness.

HARJO   Yes, it depends on your viewpoint what wilderness is. For some the city is a wilderness of concrete and steel, made within a labyrinth of mind.

LC   You mentioned before you are not only a poet, but you're a scriptwriter for television and film. How does the process work in translating your poetical world from one medium to another?

HARJO   Screenwriting is definitely related to poetry. You're dealing again with the translation of emotions into images. There's a similar kind of language involved. One goal I have, a life goal in terms of the cinema, is to create a film with a truly tribal vision, viewpoint, in terms of story, camera viewpoints, angles, everything. It hasn't been done, not on the scale I would like to do it.

LC   What do you think of non-Indian critics of your work and of Indian literature in general?

HARJO   That question could be answered many ways—I mean, there are specific non-Indian critics who get into trying to be Indian, when they don't have to. What I write, what any of us write, or are after, whether we are Indian, Chicano, Laotian, is shimmering language, poetry, the same as anyone else who is writing in whatever language; with whatever sensibilities. Or too often they won't approach the literature at all, won't read it or speak of it because, again, that guilt enters in, or that fear that keeps them from entering any place other than what is most familiar.

            As far as the literature goes, I've seen much growth in these last several years, in all of us. We are setting high standards for ourselves, our own standards, mind you, in terms of what is possible with this language, and with what we have come to know as artists of this continent.

LC   What writers are important to you?

HARJO   I consider first the writers who got me turned on to writing, what writing could do. Because I was rather a late bloomer in this business, I was never turned on by conventional English-language poetry. These writers include Simon Ortiz, Leslie Silko, and many black American writers, like June Jordan, later Audre Lorde and Alice Walker. Also Pablo Neruda, James Wright, Galway Kinnell, and African writers. I love the work of Amos Tutuola, especially *The Palm Wine Drunkard*. And there are many others.

LC   Do you see any changes in your work?

HARJO   Yes, many. If I didn't see them, didn't see growth, then I wouldn't do it any more. There are leaps between *What Moon Drove Me to This?* and *She Had Some Horses*, and I expect the leap to be huge between *Horses* and this next collection I am working on. I feel like I am just now learning how to write a poem. It has taken me over ten years to get to this point of just beginning.

LC   And what about in terms of technique?

HARJO   I'm certainly much more involved with process, inner travel, when I write now than even five years ago.

LC   Can you speak a bit more about these new poems?

HARJO   For one thing they are not so personal. I am in them, for I believe poets have to be inside their poems somewhere, or the poem won't work. But they aren't so personally revealing, and the space has grown larger. The first book was definitely centered in Oklahoma, or New Mexico. Then, in *Horses*, there was much more traveling, and in the new work [*In Mad Love and War*], there is even more traveling into the inner landscape.

LC   So, in comparison with the other books, how could you define this new book?

HARJO   Oh, it's hard to say—intensity. I would hope it is more powerful, stirring. "We Must Call a Meeting" is one of the newest poems in it. I'll read what I have, but I might change some of it.

WE MUST CALL A MEETING

I am fragile, a piece of pottery smoked from fire
                                    made of dung,
the design drawn from nightmares. I am an arrow, painted
                                    with lightning

to seek the way to the name of the enemy,
                                but the arrow has now created
its own language.
                        It is a language of lizards and storms, and we have
begun to hold conversations
                        long into the night.
                                        I forget to eat
I don't work. My children are hungry and the animals who live
in the backyard are starving.
                        I begin to draw maps of stars.
The spirits of old and new ancestors perch on my shoulders.
I make prayers of clear stone
                        of feathers from birds
                                who live closest to the gods.
The voice of the stone is born
                        of a meeting of yellow birds
who circle the ashes of smoldering ashes.
                        The feathers sweep the prayers up
and away.
                I, too, try to fly but get caught in the crossfire of signals
                        and my spirit drops back down to earth.
I am lost; I am looking for you
        who can help me walk this thin line between the breathing
                                and the dead.
You are the curled serpent in the pottery of nightmares.
You are the dreaming animal who paces back and forth in my head.
We must call a meeting.
                        Give me back my language and build a house
inside it.
        A house of madness.
                A house for the dead who are not dead.
And the spiral of the sky above it.
And the sun
        and the moon.
                And the stars to guide us called promise.

from *In Mad Love and War*

HARJO   Also another new poem, called "Transformations," about turn-
         ing someone's hatred into love. I tried to actually work that
         transformation in the poem.

TRANSFORMATIONS

This poem is a letter to tell you that I have smelled the hatred you have
tried to find me with; you would like to destroy me. Bone splintered in the
eye of one you choose to name your enemy won't make it better for you to
see. It could take a thousand years if you name it that way, but then, to see
after all that time, never could anything be so clear. Memory has many
forms. When I think of early winter I think of a blackbird laughing in the
frozen air; guards a piece of light. I saw the whole world caught in that
sound, the sun stopped for a moment because of tough belief. I don't know
what that has to do with what I am trying to tell you except that I know
you can turn a poem into something else. This poem could be a bear
treading the far northern tundra, smelling the air for sweet alive meat. Or a
piece of seaweed stumbling in the sea. Or a blackbird, laughing. What I
mean is that hatred can be turned into something else, if you have the right
words, the right meanings, buried in that tender place in your heart where
the most precious animals live. Down the street an ambulance has come to
rescue an old man who is slowly losing his life. Not many can see that he
is already becoming the backyard tree he has tended for years, before he
moves on. He is not sad, but compassionate for the fears moving around
him.

That's what I mean to tell you. On the other side of the place you live
stands a dark woman. She has been trying to talk to you for years.
You have called the same name in the middle of a nightmare,
from the center of miracles. She is beautiful.
This is your hatred back. She loves you.

                                                    from *In Mad Love and War*

LC   It's a kind of circular design again.
HARJO   Yes.

LC   Would you describe your writing process? I understand that you revise a lot.

HARJO   I begin with the seed of an emotion, a place, and then move from there. It means hours watching the space form in the place in front of the typewriter, speaking words, listening to them, watching them form, and be crossed out, on the paper, and so on, and yes, revision. I no longer see the poem as an ending point, perhaps more the end of a journey, an often long journey that can begin years earlier, say with the blur of the memory of the sun on someone's cheek, a certain smell, an ache, and will culminate years later in a poem, sifted through a point, a lake in my heart through which language must come. That's what I work with, with my students at the university, opening that place within them of original language, which I believe must be in everyone, but not everyone can reach it.

LC   You said before that you were speaking with your students about your work as well?

HARJO   I can't separate my work, my writing, from who I am, so of course it comes into the classroom with me in one way or another.

LC   Just a piece of paper with a new poem?

HARJO   Oh no, as part of that space I teach out of, a space of intuition made up of everything I know as well as what I don't know, and I've learned in writing, and in teaching, that it is important to recognize that place, to open yourself, believing.

Linda Hogan

Born in Denver in 1947 but reared in Oklahoma, Linda Hogan explains in an autobiographical sketch her relationship with tribal culture. Her development as a writer tightly meshes with her personal development:

"My father is a Chickasaw and my mother is white, from an immigrant Nebraska family. This created a natural tension that surfaces in my work and strengthens it. And as my interest in literature increased, I realized I had also been given a background of oral literature from my father's family. I use this. It has strengthened my imagination. I find that my ideas and even my work arrangement derive from that oral source. It is sometimes as though I hear those voices when I am in the process of writing.

"School was favorable for me in that it opened up a world of literature and books previously unavailable. But many creative-writing teachers were impatient with my language and my choice of subjects. I finally had one teacher who was interested in Indian literature. Working with him gave me a freedom I had missed with many other teachers and I discovered that I had been writing for them rather than out of my own preoccupation and life."[1]

Hogan received a master's degree in English and creative writing from the University of Colorado, where she has since taught American Indian literature and creative writing. She is currently an associate professor of Native American and American studies at the University of Colorado, Boulder.

She has been Poet-in-Residence for the Oklahoma and

Colorado arts councils, and in 1980 she was the recipient of a Newberry Library Fellowship and in 1982 of a Yaddo Colony Fellowship. Her poetry has appeared in the most important anthologies devoted to Native American writers, Carriers of the Dream Wheel *(1975) and* Harper's Anthology of Twentieth-Century Native American Poetry *(1988). Among her recent collections of poems,* Eclipse *was published in 1983 and* Seeing through the Sun *in 1985. She has also published a collection of short stories,* That Horse *(1985) in collaboration with her father. In 1986 she received a National Endowment for the Arts Fellowship in fiction.* Mean Spirit, *her first novel, is due to be published in 1990. Hogan has two adopted daughters and currently lives in Colorado.*

I interviewed her on September 18, 1985, at her home in Minneapolis, a little house on a shadowy street. We had dinner together so that, in Linda's words, "we will have the chance to know each other better before the interview." And indeed I acquired a deeper feeling of her nobleness of spirit and concern for other people.

LC   In "Blessing" you say "blessed are those who listen when no one is left to speak." Is it an art hard to master?

HOGAN   Everything speaks. I have a friend, Flying Clouds, who one time said, "Some people are such good listeners the trees lean towards them to tell their secrets." I think that's true. When I wrote that poem I thought about my family that we were the last in our own blood group, the last Indian people—which wasn't true at all—but at the time I thought of Indian people as vanishing and that our stories and histories were disappearing. In some ways I got that idea from public education, from white education. They want us to believe we don't exist. I realize now that the stories are eternal. They will go on as long as there are people to speak them. And the people will always be there. The people will listen to the world and translate it into a human tongue. That is the job of the poet.

LC   "The Diary of Amanda McFadden" is the title of your latest book of poetry.

HOGAN   Well, no. That book I did in 1979 and I never did find a publisher for it.

Linda Hogan

LC   So it is still unpublished?

HOGAN   It's unpublished, yes.

LC   Amanda McFadden is a fictional member of the Oneida commu-
            nity of the Perfectionists. How did you get interested in that?

HOGAN   Writers tend to be interested in everything, but I think what
            happened was, I was taking a course in American literature and
            I read about Hawthorne being in the Brook Farm community.
            And I became interested in those northeastern communities,
            and how they formed. I read biographies from members of the
            Oneida community [New York, 1847–80]. Community life has
            always interested me. I want to know why people have so much
            trouble living together. There isn't a world community. In our
            own community we are often in crisis and life can be very dif-
            ficult for people. I liked the idea of this community that was
            spiritually linked. Furthermore they had strong ideas that didn't
            really catch on again until more modern American times. They
            were interested in birth control, and sexuality, and they talked
            about that. They worked, men and women, with each other.
            Work was not defined by sex roles. I liked their ideas about
            child-rearing. They weren't nuclear-family oriented at all. The
            children had their own place to live, and parents had freedom
            to grow as much as children did. And then I was also interested
            in how the outside community looked at the Perfectionists.
            George Bernard Shaw went in and he was very impressed with
            this living and he wrote about them. And Kenneth Rexroth years
            later was writing about the Perfectionists and the particular kind
            of sexuality they practiced. People were going in, from conser-
            vative Christian organizations, and coming out saying that they
            were evil and depraved, and that the women had sensuous lips, a
            psychological projection which tells about the repression of the
            times.
                The Perfectionists weren't oppressed. And the women wore
            pants. They were the first women in this country that had the
            freedom of not wearing so much cloth that they looked like
            pieces of furniture, unable to move. Some of the skirts the
            women wore in those days had as much as fifteen yards of fabric,
            heavy fabric, just the skirt itself.

LC   So you were interested because of those things?

HOGAN   Yes, and then when I read the biographies of the people who had grown up there, they talked about what a joy it was to live in that community. And how hard it was to go out into the other America.

LC   I have read this passage [from "The Cup"] from "The Diary of Amanda McFadden": "in hundreds of years these words will return . . . not walls, but horizons." Is this a woman's self-affirmation story?

HOGAN   Yes, in many ways, I think it is. But in 1979 I wasn't thinking along those lines. But yes, it is. Amanda McFadden, the persona, really defines herself in these ways. I wrote fictional diary entries that Amanda McFadden spoke, and poems. Her conflicts were there; she could not fit in the community in some ways. For instance, there was a poem about special love, because they believed that people need to love equally all other people, and that one of the things that created problems in communities was an elite form of love, where you take a lover or a husband, or you love your child more than you love other people, and you become exclusive. She was guilty of all those things, and she confessed that. She is very human in that way, and she affirms herself in very strong ways.

LC   Is it a sense of wholeness that makes Amanda's world so close to your Indianness?

HOGAN   In some ways; living in that kind of community is, or was, a tribal life, because I think tribes are based on a kind of common spirituality and a sense of kinship to each other, as well as to their own land bases. While our Indian nations are defined as sovereign nations, the Perfectionists were also something of a nation of their own. I couldn't say that they were like Indian people, but in some ways they were treated as outcasts and as tribal people.

LC   How did that community get along with Indian people?

HOGAN   Oneida, of course, is the land of the Oneida people. They were on tribal land to begin with. In the biographies I read, or it was said, Indian people did come into the Perfectionist community to work with the non-Indians. They occasionally bought baskets. I would say that attitudes toward Indian people were a lot like those of other white Americans at that time, like the attitudes of all white Americans still. A person's liberalism in other areas doesn't have much to do with how they view people of color. I find that's a problem here. Minneapolis has the reputation of being one of the most liberal communities around, but the racism here is very strong, much more than in other places where I have lived. But it's repressed, held under the surface. And when it comes out it's dangerous, because you don't know what's going on in people's minds.

LC   Toward blacks and Indians?

HOGAN   I'd say here there's more racism toward Indian people than toward blacks. There's not as many Hispanics or Chicano people here as in the Southwest, so I don't really know what that brand of racism is like. But for the Indian community here it is very difficult. And there are class differences within this community that cause other splits and separations.

LC   In "The Transformation of Tribalism" you describe the Bear tribe, a community of Anglo and Indian people, and the Red Wind Community, a kind of alternative to traditional tribalism and to urban isolation.[2] How does it work?

HOGAN   That's such a complicated question. I don't really see an alternative. I haven't really thought about these communities for a long time, because I did that article so long ago. I don't know if these "tribes" are still out there. I think the Bear tribe travel around now and do classes for non-Indian people in urban environments, classes on spirituality. I am not sure what I feel about this because I teach in American Indian studies at the university and I find that many of the non-Indian students are desperately searching for spirits, for their own souls, that something in the contemporary world has left many Euro-Americans and Europeans without a source, has left them with a longing for something they believe existed in earlier times or in tribal people. What they want is their own life, their own love for the earth, but when they speak their own words about it, they don't believe them, so they look to Indians, forgetting that enlightenment can't be found in a weekend workshop, forgetting that most Indian people are living the crisis of American life, the toxins of chemical waste, the pain of what is repressed in white Americans. There is not such a thing as becoming an instant shaman, an instant healer, an instantly spiritualized person. Instant coffee is more likely. Pinch-bean coffee, grown right up north on the reservation. Did you read Vizenor's instant-coffee story? Now that coffee is a good way to wake up, to "waken" in the way the great and true masters of all nations speak about.

LC   Are you speaking about white shamanism?

HOGAN   Yes. That's a very large movement, and you probably noticed that, especially here and in California. It's gotten so predominant that the facts of Indian life are overlooked. My friend Shelly, a Grand Portage Indian, said that in a lot of ways it was like looking at Jews in concentration camps and saying, "Oh, aren't they beautiful people and isn't Jewish mysticism wonderful." First of all it's a theft, and it speaks a lot about the bankruptcy of other religious traditions and the need to renovate them.

LC   Would you speak about your unpublished novel, "Solar Storms"?

HOGAN   It is a book about two Indian women, sisters, and how they grow. It is also about their mother and grandmother, about love and tragedy. Roberta, one of the sisters, becomes a healer, quite by accident, and not by any tricks of instant waking, but by hard work, by loss, by learning from life about pain and hurt, death and wisdom. This is how it is done for Indian women. And Okah, the other sister, goes off to cities, travels, learns from books, and she tells the story of Roberta in a wonderful and energetic voice, tells also her own story of an Indian woman living in the contemporary world, her work, her own losses, the anger she has at being one of the unwanted.

But a novel is surely "women's work"—as my mother used to say, it is never done. In some ways the book is autobiographical. I live these two separate lives; they are both in me. Both characters represent a certain part of myself. Roberta is definitely an Oklahoma Indian woman who just experiences her life. She just lives her life the way life presents itself. Her sister leaves home and goes to California, goes to the city and learns all these new things. So they are together in the book. One lives life, the other one talks about it and lives it at the same time. They make this really wonderful new whole book. I'm enjoying it. It has a lot of humor in it. They both reach the same place but they do it in very different ways.

LC   You said that there is a lot of humor in it. Speaking of humor, I think it is one of the most important features in modern American Indian literature. Can you speak about that—humor in the modern stories and humor in the old ones? Is there any difference?

HOGAN   In some ways when I think about [Gerald] Vizenor's work, it has a lot of humor in it. His humor maybe comes from some traditional background, but also he's an educated man. He has a pretty critical mind and he thinks about things, and sees through a lot of things that are taking place. He sees through the surface, and that's where his humor comes from. But where I come from, in my family, and in my particular tribe, people are always funny and joking around and teasing, using very rich language. My uncle once said—he plays the fiddle—he said he couldn't read music because it looked like a bunch of crows on a telephone line. He'd say things like how Mildred was about as surprised as when Aunt Bell's bloomers fell down. There's just a lot of humor all the time. Things are funny. It's a survival technique, too. People who are in poverty, people who are in very difficult situations and in pain, have to develop humor or die of despair.

LC   Like Coyote [the Trickster character in Indian mythology].

HOGAN   Yes, yes. The two-sided part of it. I have had to develop more humor, since I've been here. Even in public, like when I am doing public presentations, because after the first twenty times somebody tells you that they were reincarnated Indians, you have to have a humorous perspective or you are going to put somebody up against the wall.

LC   So there is a lot of humor in your new novel, still in progress.

HOGAN   Yes. I am working on a section called "We loved Job." My friend Priscilla Garrigan and I were sitting over coffee one night, talking about our histories, and she said that they had loved Job. I said, yes, so did we, but I wouldn't have said it like that, and could I borrow the line for my book? Anyway, the characters in this section are talking about how they grew up on Job. Then they begin analyzing that Job didn't really fight back and they end up by observing that they aren't at all like Job and maybe he was kind of passive, and so on. I build from there and it has a lot of humor.

LC   What about American Indian writers and publishing?

HOGAN   I'm sure everyone has told you the same thing on this question. I think it's easier for a non-Indian to write a book about Indian people and get it published than it is for us. Our own experiences and our own lives don't fit the stereotypes. I think part of it is that, for non-Indian people in the United States, they really want to fit Indians into a category. If you want to write about Indian race-car drivers, they don't want to read about it, because it's not romantic and it's not interesting. It defies the categories. Our experience is denied us. Most of us publish with third-world book publishers.

LC   Is it easier to publish a book with a small press or with a big publishing house?

HOGAN   I've had really good fortune with small presses. I have not looked very much at big publishing houses, but I would like to, I would like to for my novel. I'm really interested in doing commercial writing right now. Especially after Louise Erdrich's book [*Love Medicine*] came out, or Louise and Michael's, I feel like it would really be important to earn a living from my writing, so that I could buy myself time to do more writing. When I have to work, it takes away so much writing time. I feel too that as Indian people, we deny ourselves that commercial value. I feel that with Louise, that was a great breakthrough for Indian writers, for her to succeed financially. I have mostly published with small presses because these presses would accept the work that I do, and make their facilities available. I think that is true of almost all the Indian writers now. I know that Paula [Gunn Allen] has published her novel through Spinster's Ink, a small women's press.

LC   In several of your poems, you describe the devastating consequences after the nuclear explosions of Hiroshima and Nagasaki. Are you involved in the antinuclear movement?

HOGAN   I'm not active at the time, but I've been. A lot of the work I've done, and a lot of the speaking I've done has been against that, against all war. During the Korean War my father joined the military. And so, as a child, as a young girl, I was always aware of war, because that was after the atomic bomb, and we had to hide under our desks at school. But also being in the military we had information sent to us all the time about fall-out—you boil your clothes and bathe. Plus, for as long as I can remember in my life, I have always been against violence. I have lived around a lot of violence, and I've always been a person who tries to interrupt it. It's not the best thing to do sometimes. I want peace, and I've always thought about why is it that people don't have peace, don't live in peace. So I've spent a lot of thinking time in my life, and even my fantasy life as a child, trying to decide why it is that people fight, why it is that people have war. I think that war and peace have been my occupation and my preoccupation for as long as I can remember. Spirituality necessitates certain kinds of political action. If you believe that the earth, and all living things, and all the stones are sacred, your responsibility really is to protect those things. I do believe that's our duty, to be custodians of the planet. What has amazed me is that after the first bomb, you would have thought all war would stop forever, and that they could find a way to resolve all conflict.

I was reading recently Helen Caldicott, who wrote *Nuclear Madness*. Are you familiar with her work? She was talking about how if a bomb were now dropped here, with the kinds of bombs we have now, the new ones, it would create a crater that was three miles deep and wide; and twenty-six miles out, people would be evaporated; the ones we have now are so enormous. The bomb that was dropped on Hiroshima is just used as a trigger for those new bombs.

LC   Are you active in the American Indian Movement?

HOGAN No, I am not. I was once active with the Women of All Red Nations.

LC   What's your opinion about the impact that the American Indian movement has on Indians, just generally speaking?

HOGAN Generally speaking? I don't think there's just one impact, because there are so many different opinions. Some people think that the American Indian Movement was a wonderful form of new leadership, and other people think that it was mostly city Indians who were creating a lot of problems, that created more trouble on reservations than was necessary. I know elders who were active in the American Indian Movement, and they are spiritual leaders, traditional people. I really feel that the American Indian Movement was important and really necessary. I think it had some good consequences, but that is just my opinion. I don't want to speak for other Indian people. The publicity and attention that was gained from that movement is significant for Indian people now. Even now.

LC   In "Native American Women: Our Voice, the Air," you say that "many of the older ways infuse the new," and that "living in a complex bicultural society has vitalized culture-identity," but at the same time, "Indian women are aware of the difficult situation of being female and minority."[3] Would you elaborate on that?

HOGAN   To be a woman and be a minority woman in this country is like a double-whammy, or maybe even a triple-whammy. It's hard enough to be either one or the other. I think also here minority women and the white women's movement don't really see eye to eye very often. It's very hard in some ways to integrate those two movements. Most minority women have completely different sets of priorities. For instance, equal pay is really important for everybody, but you're looking at how some minority women haven't learned basic skills because they haven't had the opportunities that women from the dominant culture have had; you get to point A of a division. The problems are so basically different; it's like trying to break in and survive, versus trying to have a position equal to a white man in a corporation. The priorities there are very different. The issues are very different. I don't mean to minimize the women's movement, but it seems to me that there are many women's movements now.

LC   Are American Indian women active in women's organizations?

HOGAN   I don't know how it is in other places, but my experience is that we are less active now than in the past, because for Indian women particularly, those organizations didn't return anything to us or to our communities. I noticed when I moved here to Minneapolis that I was very much in demand, even though I was new here, even though there are other Indian women writers here. One of the things that they do is they value me because I came in with this job [at the University of Minnesota] and suddenly I was an acceptable Indian woman writer. And the other women were not. What a separating thing to have happen. There are different values at work. Sometimes it seems we are working at cross-purposes with each other. Yet we all have things in common, and it's possible to work these things out. Like I said, some of the issues that come up are spiritual issues, and issues with racism and classism and those really separate people; they really divide us from each other. And I need to retreat for a long time to think this through, to see if bridges can be formed between these islands.

LC   How did acculturation change American Indian women's lifestyle?

HOGAN   It's been devastating. It's such a big consideration, it's hard to begin talking about it. Look at just one system within the other systems. If you look at the [boarding school] educational system, and how for tribal people, to be taken away from home as a young child; to have the whole family system and the tribal system broken up by children being taken away from families— you can imagine the consequences it still has on families even now. It's almost as if we have to reeducate ourselves to be families again, to be mothers. That is just one system. What does it do to take a child away from family. Not to be able to bond with anyone, to be completely separate, not to get any physical affection. Psychologically, the damage is very severe and that's just one aspect. There's all this romanticization of Indians on the one hand, and yet there's so much crisis on the other hand. Not just poverty, but a lot of abuse; there's a rising number of sexual abuses and physical abuses, of child battery, on Indian territory. Once a people are victims, they have to struggle hard to politicize themselves and to be able to break the cycle, to be able to somehow, as they say today, to empower themselves once again, to get back their health and their wholeness. It is made doubly hard by the fact that it was close to us, but we have to pull together the energy to get whole.

LC   Do American Indian people see the writer's work as a means to preserve their own culture?

HOGAN   Ideally, it would be nice to say yes, that's true, and it has been that way in the past, and I think at this time the other issues affecting Indian people are so severe that art is a luxury, despite Audre Lorde's essay "Poetry Is Not a Luxury."[4]

LC   Does literature develop a sense of Pan-Indianness?

Linda Hogan

HOGAN   Yes, it does. One of the things that has happened is that people
         have been able to see that their experience as an Indian person is
         not so unique. It's not an individual thing but is shared by people
         in other communities. Also, we all know each other, so there's
         this Pan-Indian identity as an Indian writer. When new people
         come along, we learn from them, and they learn from us, and
         everybody gets together in a larger circle. Some things kind of
         get passed through, like a relay race, but I also see that everyone
         is working very individually, too, on their own things. I know
         since I came here I am writing a lot of city poems, writing a lot
         about what it's like to be in this kind of community. Minneapo-
         lis is a very racist place. Some of the events that are really major
         against Indians which happen here I incorporate into my book.
         If there's police brutality, I write about it.

LC   What do you think of non-Indian critics and readers of your work
         and of American Indian literature in general?

HOGAN   To tell the truth I have two feelings about that. One is that I feel
         very possessive about our work. But the other is that the non-
         Indian readers and critics have been crucial and important for
         getting our work out and distributed. There are some very good
         non-Indian people doing research on Indian literature.

LC   Would you describe your writing process?

HOGAN   I do my best work when I can be quiet, and when I can be open
         and let the process take over and do the work for me. I used to
         say that the earth writes through me, but since I have lived here,
         my writing is a little bit more head writing for now: I hope that's
         temporary.

LC   Have you been influenced by any writer?

HOGAN   I have been influenced by all of them. I read everything I get my
         hands on. And I'm influenced by trees, weather, dreams, insects,
         sun.

LC   Any major influence?

HOGAN   I love Pablo Neruda. I think when I first read Momaday's *House
         Made of Dawn* I thought it was for me the most important thing
         I had read. I also used to hear Elizabeth Bishop called poets' poet,
         so I always read her work very carefully and I liked her work a
         great deal. I was talking about the writing process—if I can be
         quiet somehow I feel that I can trap a great energy, and that's
         really the major influence on what I do. I also find it important

82

to keep up with reading and I read a lot of work from other countries, a lot of work in translation, and I like to keep a finger on the pulse of the whole world.

LC   Do you have any work in progress right now?

HOGAN   Yes, I am finishing a book of poems and I have a novel in progress. The book of poems consists of city poems, mostly. They have a lot of humor and a faster language than I've done in the other work.

LC   What do you mean by "faster language"?

HOGAN   They have a little bit more jargon; the pace is a little more clipped, and sped up. They have more humor. I'm working on very lively things right now. I use a cliché and then I use it against itself.

LC   So can you say that your work has somehow evolved in terms of interest and craft?

HOGAN   The interest is the same, but the craft is different, yes. Actually, I don't think I can shake those things that are in my personal universe. What I have been doing is finding new ways of saying the same old things. These poems are very political, but on the surface they don't sound like it. Once you look at them, they are very intense.

LC   You have some new poems that will be published in the new edition of Duane Niatum's *Harper's Anthology of Twentieth-Century Native American Poetry* [1988]. Would you read some of them?

THE NEW APARTMENT, MINNEAPOLIS

The floorboards creak.
The moon is on the wrong side of the building,

and burns remain
on the floor.

The house wants to fall down
the universe when earth turns.

It still holds the coughs of old men
and their canes tapping on the floor.

Linda Hogan

I think of Indian people here before me
and how last spring white merchants hung an elder

on a meathook and beat him;
he was one of The People.

I remember this war
and all the wars

and relocation like putting the moon in prison
with no food and that moon was a crescent

but be warned, the moon grows full again
and the roofs of this town are all red

and we are looking through the walls of houses
at people suspended in air.

Some are baking, with flour on their hands,
or sleeping on floor three, or getting drunk.

I see the business men who hit their wives
and the men who are tender fathers.

There are women crying or making jokes.
Children are laughing under beds.

Girls in navy blue robes talk on the phone all night
and some Pawnee is singing 49's, drumming the table.

Inside the walls
world changes are planned, bosses overthrown.

If we had no coffee,
cigarettes or liquor,

says the woman in room 12,
they'd have a revolution on their hands.

Beyond walls are lakes and plains,
canyons and the universe;

the stars are the key
turning in the lock of night.

Linda Hogan

Turn the deadbolt and I am home.
I have walked to the dark earth,

opened a door to nights where there are no apartments,
just drumming and singing;

The Duck Song, The Snake Song,
The Drunk Song.

No one here remembers the city
or has ever lost the will to go on.

Hello aunt, hello brothers, hello trees
and deer walking quietly on the soft red earth.

LC   Would you read the other poem, "Workday"?

HOGAN Yes. This is a poem about seeing people every day in the city
and being new here, and thinking about all the concerns I have
had in my life and how hard it is to talk about them, here, in the
city, where people are hustling. This is a fast place. A friend of
mine calls it a "Hurry up and get there city."

WORKDAY

I go to work
though there are those who were missing today
from their homes.
I ride the bus
and I do not think of children without food
or how my sisters are chained to prison beds.
I go to the university
and out for lunch
and listen to the higher ups
tell me all they have read
about Indians
and how to analyze this poem.
They know us
better than we know ourselves.

Linda Hogan

I ride the bus home
and sit behind the driver.
We talk about the weather
and not enough exercise.
I don't mention Victor Jara's mutilated hands
or men next door
in exile
or my own family's grief over the lost child.

When I get off the bus
I look back at the light in the windows
and the heads bent
and how the women are all alone
in each seat
framed in the windows
and the men are coming home,
then I see them walking on the Avenue,
the beautiful feet,
the perfect legs
even with their spider veins,
the broken knees
with pins in them,
the thighs with their cravings,
the pelvis
and small back
with its soft down,
the shoulders which bend forward
and forward and forward
to protect the heart from pain.

N. Scott Momaday

N. Scott Momaday was born in 1934 at Lawton, Oklahoma. His father, Al Momaday, a Kiowa, was an accomplished artist, and for many years he was principal of the day school at the Pueblo of Jemez, New Mexico. His mother, Natachee Scott, of Cherokee descent, is a well-known writer, painter, and teacher, educated at Haskell Institute in Lawrence, Kansas, and then at the University of New Mexico.

When Momaday was two, the family left Oklahoma and lived in various places in the Southwest, especially in the Navajo country. In 1946 they moved to the Pueblo of Jemez, a Towa-speaking village, where Momaday's parents were each offered teaching positions. He attended high school in Santa Fe and Albuquerque and, in his final year, at Augustus Military Academy, Fort Defiance, Virginia. In 1958 he received his bachelor's degree in political science from the University of New Mexico.

Urged by a friend to apply for the Wallace Stegner Creative Scholarship at Stanford University, he won the award and began to study under Yvor Winters. Momaday received his doctoral degree in 1963; his dissertation, on Frederick Goddard Tuckerman's poetry, was published two years later. After his doctoral degree, he taught English and comparative literature at the University of California at Santa Barbara and Berkeley, Stanford University, and the University of Arizona, Tucson, where he currently teaches and lives. He is the father of three daughters.

The Journey of Tai-Me, *privately printed in Santa Barbara in 1967, was his first publication devoted to the mythical lore of the Kiowa. It was followed in 1968 by* House Made of Dawn, *which won the 1969 Pulitzer Prize. This success marked the beginning of a new Native American literature and paved the way for young Indian writers.* The Way to Rainy Mountain *(1969) continues Momaday's journey into his tribal past, a journey which is defined by the writer himself in that book as "The history of an idea, man's idea of himself."*[1]

The Names *(1976) is an autobiographical account shaping his own Indian identity and giving voice to his personal past. His poetry has appeared in two collections,* Angle of Geese and Other Poems *(1974) and* The Gourd Dancer *(1976). His many essays, short prose, and articles witness his commitment to issues concerning Indian culture. Some of them, widely anthologized, are exceptional assessments of Native American thought, as indicated by a selection of titles: "The Man Made of Words," "An American Land Ethic," "A First American Views His Land," "The Morality of Indian Hating," "Native American Attitudes toward the Environment."*

In the past few years Momaday has also gained an increasingly high reputation as a painter: in 1979 he had his first show at the University of North Dakota, and since then he has exhibited in Minneapolis; Norman, Oklahoma; Santa Fe, New Mexico; Phoenix, Tucson, and Scottsdale, Arizona; Basel; and Heidelberg.

The interview took place on September 25, 1985, at Momaday's house, on the outskirts of Tucson. Some of the desert plants surrounding the area were still in full bloom, brilliant and colorful against the gray lightness of the sand. Once inside, his imposing yet warm voice quietly took hold of the room.

LC   The understanding of the landscape is one of the most important aspects of Indian oral tradition. As you said, "I should affirm myself in the spirit of the land," or just to use one of your favorite expressions in defining this relationship, "There are places where you have *invested* your life,"[2] but you suggest that there is also a process of appropriation. Would you elaborate on that?

MOMADAY Well, yes, I think that the sense of place is very important in American Indian oral tradition. And the question is how does one acquire such a sense and I think it is a long process of appropriation. The American Indian has a very long experience of the North American continent, say, going back thousands of years, maybe thirty thousand. So I think of that as being a very great investment, a kind of spiritual investment in the landscape, and because he has that experience he is able to think of himself in a particular way, think of himself in relation to the land, and he is able to define for himself a sense of place, belonging, and to me that is very important and characterizes much of the American Indian oral tradition. Probably writing too, more recently, because the writing, I think, springs in a natural way from the oral tradition and the sense of place is crucial to both.

LC And does it work this way in literature?

MOMADAY Literature at large?

LC Yes.

MOMADAY I think so. I think that in most literature that I know of, the sense of place is important. It differs, of course; when I talk about the American Indian and his many thousands of years in America, I think of that as a unique experience, but certainly there are other unique experiences in other parts of the world and involving other peoples. But the sense of place, I think, across the board, is important in literature.

LC But could you say that the spirit of the place is better interpreted and understood in literature by western and southern writers? I am speaking of American literature.

MOMADAY Talking about American Indian literature, certainly the center of that literature is in the West, I think, because the oldest surviving societies are in the West. We have communities of people in Arizona, New Mexico, Nevada, Montana, and so on, whose way of life has continued in a way that is not so of other parts of the country. I don't know, I can't really speak to the Northeast as a geographical area; I just don't know enough about it, but I do know that the oral tradition, the Indian oral tradition is very strong in the West, and in American literature exclusive of Native American literature the tradition seems to be very strong in the South.

LC   Can you see any difference between these two approaches, be-
            tween the western and the southern?

MOMADAY   Yes, sure. I think of southern literature as focusing largely upon
            the War Between the States and the development before that
            war, of an agrarian society in the South, which was aristocratic
            in large measure, and then the collapse of that society.

LC   Decadent, white society.

MOMADAY   Yes. Faulkner of course is the person who comes to mind as
            the spokesman of that ideal; and he says something to the ef-
            fect in one of his books that for every boy who grows up in the
            South and so on, there is still that moment at Gettysburg. But
            the West, on the other hand, the western literature deals with
            another question, and that is the opening of the frontier, which
            in a sense, I think, is still going on. So that in one way the lit-
            erature of the West is newer, I think, than the literature of the
            South; it deals with a more recent and ongoing experience in the
            American imagination. I am fond of dealing with the history of
            the West and the imaging of the West in the American mind. I
            think it's a rich kind of field to explore. The American Indian
            experience is part of that as well.

LC   As you yourself said, *House Made of Dawn* is very symmetrical.
            Is it a design coming out from the cultural world in which the
            events take place?

MOMADAY   Yes, I think so. I think that the novel reflects a kind of shape
            that is real in the American Indian world.

LC   *The Names* is the title of your memoir. In one of your poems
            the carriers of the dream wheel "spin the names of the earth and
            sky."[3] Thus is language, in shaping "the aboriginal names," the
            first creative act?

MOMADAY   Is it the first creative act? Probably, probably. I think there is in-
            herent in the Native American worldview the idea that naming
            is coincidental with creation; that, when you bestow a name
            upon someone or something you at the same time invest it with
            being. It's not an idea, by the way, that's peculiar to Native
            American experience; it's a worldwide kind of idea, but it is cer-
            tainly important in American Indian society. And I think, yes,
            this is where things begin—naming.

LC   "A man's name is his own." Even the dead take their names with
            them.

MOMADAY   Yes, that's true in certain American Indian societies, the Kiowa is what I had in mind. That was true of that society; when someone died in the tribe he was thought to take his name with him, out of the world, unless he had given it away before he died and that frequently happened. It was a great honor to be given a name, someone's name.

LC   So the investment of the self in the spirit of the land, and the investment of the self in language.

MOMADAY   Yes, yes, I think so.

LC   And how can the written language continue and develop the oral tradition?

MOMADAY   It's not a question that one can answer quickly or simply, but it seems to me that the things that inform oral tradition, the very best oral tradition, are the things that ought to inform the best literature, the best of the written tradition. In other words I think that the two traditions are probably more apparently different than they are really different, one from the other. At some point they converge, and they share, I think, the same qualities. And the storyteller in the oral tradition is doing—or maybe better to put it the other way round—the writer who is writing a novel, say, is engaged in pretty much the same activity, it seems to me, as the storyteller who is telling a story in the oral tradition. There are differences, of course, but in the main, I think, they are probably closer together than we realize.

LC   What's the real relationship, the essence of their relationship?

MOMADAY   Well, the writer, like the storyteller, I think, is concerned to create himself and his audience in language. That's probably the most important single common denominator. Both are acts of creation and so are in some sense indivisible.

LC   So we have storyteller-audience, writer-reader.

MOMADAY   Yes. And that relationship, between the storyteller and the listener, is pretty much the same relationship as that between the writer and the reader, with some obvious distinctions.

LC   There are recurrent patterns in contemporary American Indian literature. Do you think that we can speak then of some common denominators?

MOMADAY   Well, what occurs to me is that all of modern American Indian writing, it seems to me, proceeds from the same national experience, if I can put it that way. It proceeds from the same general history and prehistory; that is to say, I think that one of the things that characterizes or ought to characterize American Indian literature is a procession from the oral tradition. Oral tradition is at the root of modern American Indian literature, and everybody, every Indian who is writing out of his Indianness, I think, has that in mind, whether consciously or not; but he is working with precedents that go back into oral tradition.

LC   In *Ceremony* and *House Made of Dawn*, for instance, the main characters are both veterans coming back from their war experience and both of them become "inarticulate" in that they can't speak or communicate to other people. I am not speaking just in terms of a literature coming out from the oral tradition, but of themes, characters, events.

MOMADAY   Well, the figure—I can speak about *House Made of Dawn*—of Abel is commonplace in the sense that he is a kind of, a kind of —I can't think of the word I want—he represents a great many people of his generation, the Indian who returns from the war, the Second World War. He is an important figure in the whole history of the American experience in this country. It represents such a dislocation of the psyche in our time. Almost no Indian of my generation or of Abel's generation escaped that dislocation, that sense of having to deal immediately with, not only with the traditional world, but with the other world which was placed over the traditional world so abruptly and with great violence. Abel's generation is a good one to write about, simply because it's a tragic generation. It is not the same, the generation after Abel did not have the same experience, nor the one before. So it is, in some sense, the logical one to deal with in literature.

LC   Yes. There are always three generations in, and the main characters come out from the third generation.

MOMADAY   Yes, Yes.

LC   It being understood that individual tribal thought and traditions are indispensable in analyzing structure and content of these works because they come from very different cultural worlds.

MOMADAY   Exactly. That's right. That's very important, very important.

LC   Do you feel that in your prose poems there is a stronger link with the oral tradition?

MOMADAY   I think that the prose poems are very close to oral tradition, to

Indian oral tradition, and probably closer than most of the poems that are composed in verse. The oral tradition of the Indian has a closer model, represents a closer model, for the prose poem than for the poem. It's storytelling traditions, and it's in one sense easier to tell a story in a prose poem than in a poem.

LC   In 1970 you wrote in "Learning from the Indian" that "more than ever before, the Indian is in possession of his future as well as of his past" and that "he stands to make a major contribution to the modern world" in terms of "Indian land ethic, his integrity as a man and a race, capacity for wonder, delight and belief."[4] Contemporary American Indian literature is playing a remarkable role in American literature at large, it's a very innovating contribution to it. Is American Indian literature a major vehicle for that?

MOMADAY   Yes, I think so, because the Indian has always had such a keen regard for language. So literature as such is a large part of his experience and one of his great contributions, I think. And you are right, the American Indian literature is becoming a very important, recognizably important, part of American literature as a whole. And we are just now rethinking the boundaries of American literature, and we are obliged, I think, to include oral tradition, elements of oral tradition, that we did not even think of including twenty-five years ago.

LC   And just in terms of contributions, what's the major contribution to American literature at large?

MOMADAY   That whole oral tradition which goes back probably to beyond the invention of the alphabet; the storyteller was the man who was standing with a piece of charcoal in his hand making, placing, the wonderful images in his mind's eye on the wall of the cave, that's probably one of the origins of American literature. He has begun to tell a story, and he develops in the course of time that storytelling capacity in himself to such a wonderful degree that we have to recognize it as being somewhere in the line, in the evolution of what we think of American literature. I have an idea that American literature really begins with the first human expression of man in the American landscape, and who knows how far back that goes; but it certainly antedates writing, and it probably goes back a thousand years or more. So we have to admit it now, and always think in terms of it. We cannot think of Melville without thinking of American Indian antecedents in the oral tradition, because the two things are not to be separated logically at all.

LC   What about language and imagery?

MOMADAY   I think there is a close correlation: before a man could write, he could draw; but writing is drawing, and so the image and the word cannot be divided.

LC   Now to speak about structure. As you said before, the structure of your novel *House Made of Dawn* comes out from your cultural world.

MOMADAY   That's right. That's right.

LC   So there is also a major contribution in terms of technique.

MOMADAY   Yes, I am sure of that.

LC   Writing on white-Indian relations in 1964, you stated that "the morality of intolerance has become in the twentieth century a morality of pity" and that the contemporary white American, on the whole, is ambiguous and even contradictory with respect to Indians.[5] In your opinion, is there any significant change more than twenty years later?

MOMADAY   Yes, I think so. I think that the morality of pity has given way to something else.

LC   So there is another stage?

MOMADAY   There is another stage. Maybe a present and ongoing stage. The Indian has made remarkable strides in the direction of assimilation. He gets along in the larger world beyond the boundaries of the reservation much better now than he did twenty years ago. He has made tremendous strides in that respect and he has made them without having to sacrifice, I think, his most intrinsic and important values. He remains an Indian, which is the whole point of it. He brings his Indianness, as he always has, really, with him into new experiences, into new territories. There was at one time a real danger. The Indian simply being frozen as an image in the American mind. But I think we have largely dislodged that image and he becomes something also more vital and infinitely more adaptable than the figure on the screen who is being chased by John Wayne.

LC   You are a writer and a painter as well, like your father. Quite a number of American Indian writers are also painters. Do you think that there is a special reason for it? Is it because there is a remarkable aesthetic perception in the Indian universe?

MOMADAY I think that's part of it and I think also that the real answer to it probably lies in the very thing we were talking about a moment ago, the proximity of the image and the word to things. In one sense the painter is doing what the writer is doing; that is, he's constructing images that represent reality in one way or another, and when you start to think about it that's what the writer does too. He constructs images that represent reality. Words are artificial in the way that paint on canvas is artificial; it's not the real world; it's a reflection, one remove from the real world, and in some ways the reflection is truer than the things it represents as it passes through the intelligence of the painter or of the writer. But the activities, the two activities, seem to me very much alike.

LC Speaking of modern Indian painters such as R. C. Gorman, C. F. Lovato, Harry Fonseca, Fritz Scholder, T. C. Cannon, Neil Parsons, can you see in their subjects, color techniques, any connections with contemporary American Indian writers?

MOMADAY Sure. Yes. Lots of them. If you take for one example Jim Welch's *Winter in the Blood*, you can find that story or that narrative illustrated in the work of Fritz Scholder. I can think of, I can bring to mind paintings and prints that Fritz has made which might very well illustrate a passage in Welch. And I think that's probably true of a great many painters and writers. They are dealing with the same subjects in obvious ways.

LC What about your own paintings?

MOMADAY I am late to come to painting. I've only been at it for about twelve years, seriously painting. And I'm still feeling my way. I have come from more or less abstract images and drawing to something else; I have recently taken up watercolor for the first time, and I find it terribly exacting to work in watercolor. It's very different from acrylics with which I have been working for some years, and before that, ink-and-brush work on paper, drawing in a real sense. So it's hard for me to talk about my painting because it seems to me in flux at the moment. I don't know where it is, where it's going.

LC   Just in progress.

MOMADAY But it is in progress. And I feel very good about that, and I feel that I am coming closer to realizing whatever talent I have for painting as I go. And that's always a good sense, you know, a sense of accomplishment.

LC   What do you think of the non-Indian critics of your work and of American Indian literature in general?

MOMADAY Well, I don't know. I think that critics are critics whether they are looking at American Indian writing or painting or whatever. It's like everything else, some critics are wonderfully astute and intelligent and others are wonderfully stupid. So the writer and the painter, I think, had best ignore the critics as far as they can. Too much praise is bad for the writer or the painter and certainly negative reception of his work is an impairment too. I don't pay much attention to people who write glowing things about my work because I think that can be deceptive, it can get in my way, and I pay even less attention to people who take me to task, for one reason or another, because that too gets in my way. It's rather nice to work with blinds on, if you know what I mean, and profitable, I think.

LC   What about the critical reception of your work in Europe?

MOMADAY Well, it's been very gratifying, I think. I am always a little amazed when I read things that have been written about my work, and I think I can say that most of what has been written about my work has been altogether favorable, and of course that's the way I would have it. But on the other hand, you know, I think, to repeat myself, I think that for me anyway, it's best to keep working and to pay not so much attention to what people have said about what I have done in the past.

LC   How has your work evolved in the past few years?

MOMADAY Oh, I think I just spoke to that point with respect to painting. I don't know, it's hard for me to see, hard for me to look at my own work and draw any conclusions about it. The novel that I am writing is not like anything I have written before, so that it represents some sort of new direction in my work, I think. It's contemporary in the main, but it does draw a lot upon historical facts and prehistoric, mythological elements. So that it covers a wide range of things. It is basically the story about a man, and the setting is for the most part in the present, but there are a lot of references to, as I said, to things in the past. It has got an Indian character to it, but has also got a kind of non-Indian dimension to it. The principal character is an Indian who does not know he is an Indian, and part of the story has to do with his finding out he is an Indian, what it means to him. But in any case I can't talk much about it because probably I am not even half through it yet, and so I have no idea what it's going to become. I'm happy with what it is now; it's fun working on it, gratifying to work on it, but it's too early to describe it in any real way.

LC   Would you describe your writing process?

MOMADAY Well, I think of myself as being a very undisciplined kind of writer. I have moments of inspiration: I never know when they are going to come upon me, and when they do I try to take advantage of them. I write now in the early part of the day, when I am really rolling along. I like to get up early and get to work early, and I can work, I find, for maybe six hours at the most, writing, and then I have to back away and do something else; but if I can write, say, four hours a day consistently, that's as much as I ask of myself.

LC   Do you have any book of poetry in progress?

MOMADAY Well, I have some poems which have not been published, several poems, maybe half a dozen; and these are, I hope, to be part of a forthcoming book, but I write poetry so slowly that I don't even envision a book of poems by a certain date. It will happen when it happens, that's all I can say. But I like some of the recent poems I have written and so I keep that going too, you know, in addition to the painting and the novel.

LC   Is there an evolution as a poet as well?

MOMADAY Yes. I started off writing poetry without knowing what poetry was and so it was very ragged. Then I went to study under a man who knew a great deal about poetic forms and he taught me a lot, and I changed; my writing changed under his teaching, so that it became much more clearly defined in traditional ways.

LC   You are speaking of Winters?

MOMADAY Yes, Yvor Winters. And then when I left Stanford and after Winters had retired and then died, my writing of poems changed again, I think, and it became freer. I had backed myself into a corner and I was so conscious of the traditional English forms of poetry that I left myself very little place to maneuver. So I opened up a bit and my verse became freer, not free verse, not entirely free, but more flexible, I think. I keep writing in that more flexible way, though now that I think about it, it's rather interesting to me that of the maybe last six poems I have written, at least two of them are sonnets, the very tightly controlled forms. But I have achieved, I think, in those traditional forms, a kind of freedom that I did not have before. So that's probably to the good.

Simon Ortiz

One of the best-known contemporary Native American poets, Simon Ortiz was born at the Pueblo of Acoma, New Mexico, in 1941. After attending high school he worked in the uranium mines and processing plants of the Grants Ambrosia Lake area, quitting that job after a year. He went to college to be a chemist, although at that time he had already decided to devote himself to writing. He left the college and enlisted in the U.S. Army, mainly to see new places and meet people. After his army service, he enrolled in 1966 as a student at the University of New Mexico and began to publish some poems in small magazines. Later he received an M.F.A. degree from the University of Iowa. He has taught creative writing and Native American literature at California State University, San Diego; the University of New Mexico; and Sinte Gleska College, Rosebud, South Dakota.

He has three children and currently lives at Acoma Pueblo. He has been appointed lieutenant-governor of the pueblo and is now serving his people in this office.

In addition to being a teacher, Ortiz has also been a journalist, public relations director, and editor of a community newspaper. As a result of his work as a writer and journalist, Ortiz received in 1969 a Discovery Award from the National Endowment for the Arts.

Ortiz points out that although his writing was rooted in his Native American heritage and oral tradition, it was also stimulated by the social and political climate of the 1960s. At that time his work was more than ever concerned about expressing a tribal literary voice: "It was revolutionary, at least to me, to write about my culture, history, and heritage, especially since there was nothing, not even a tiny bit of it, from a Native perspective in previous works of literature"[1]

His book of poetry From Sand Creek *(1981) received the Pushcart Prize for Poetry. Other recent publications include* Fightin': New and Collected Stories *(1983) and* Earth Power Coming *(1983), a widely praised anthology of Native American short fiction.*

On September 20, 1985, I reached him in Mission, South Dakota, in the heart of Rosebud Indian Reservation, where at that time he was teaching creative writing at Sinte Gleska College. A few houses flanked the dusty road. A little shopping center, although animated and fairly crowded, didn't break the pervasive sense of isolation and poverty. We met at the place where I was staying and talked all afternoon. Then we said goodbye, shaking hands at the doorway. He went toward his car. I stood watching, still feeling the strength of his Indian culture and the tribal commitment of his poetical voice.

LC   Would you talk about the storytelling tradition and its importance to you as a writer?

ORTIZ   The oral tradition is not just speaking and listening, because what it means to me and to other people who have grown up in that tradition is that whole process, that whole process which involves a lifestyle. That whole process of that society in terms of its history, its culture, its language, its values, and subsequently, its literature. So it's not merely a simple matter of speaking and listening, but living that process. And the oral tradition obviously includes everything within it, whether or not it's spoken about or acted out, or worked out, or how people respond to each other personally and socially. So the importance really of the oral tradition is the importance of what your philosophy is, in terms of your identity, what your heritage is, and how that forms, formulates itself in creative expression called writing. That's what it is. When I say oral tradition I mean, for myself as an Acoma person not just knowing the stories and not just knowing the songs, but how I am determined by my being born and growing

Simon Ortiz

up in the Acoma Pueblo community of New Mexico and the Southwest.

LC   How can the oral narrative style be expressed in written work?

ORTIZ   Writing for me is the utilization of language, and "the utilization of language" means referring to the oral tradition. So that the oral tradition is fundamental to how the language you learn and develop in writing then expresses itself in the contemporary period, in writing. It's not a step removed or even a bridge crossed, but actually part of that path or road or journey that you are walking. Native American people, before the European colonization of this country, were multilingual. They spoke not only their mother tongue but that of sister nations and cultures next to them. In the same sense Native American people speaking French, English, and Spanish after European colonization simply were another addition of other languages. Of course, that colonialism was in process makes a difference, obviously. Essentially, writing today is, in a sense, an acquisition of a language, extending the multilanguage ability-facility of Native American people. The Native American writing tradition being developed now is in line with the oral tradition, the utilization of language.

LC   It's also a literature deeply rooted in the spirit of place, the same spirit which informs your writing.

ORTIZ   It cannot be anything other than that place. You recognize your birth as coming from a specific place, but that place is more than just a physical or geographical place, but obviously a spiritual place, a place with the whole scheme of life, the universe, the whole scheme and power of creation. Place is the source of who you are in terms of your identity, the language that you are born into and that you come to use. English is part of that place in the sense that language is source, and if language is extended to include languages other than your own, then that sense of place would not be so different when expressed in another language. What you are connecting with is still that spiritual source, which is that place from which you stand right now.

LC   The coyote figure in your poems reveals a deep communion with the natural world. It has been said he is, above all, "Coyote, the Survivor."

ORTIZ   Unfortunately, Coyote is chosen as an easy, identifiable figure, it seems to me. Coyote is chosen simply because of the kind of character that it is, or he or she is—a character which is changeable, interchangeable, and can be identifiable, to a certain extent, with some European or Western civilization's human traits. I think that in all cultures there is some sort of figure, whether it's the raven or the fox from Aesop's *Fables*, or some other cultural storytelling figures out of Africa or Asia. There is some sort of archetypal character that can be like Coyote. The coyote, or whatever the name is given to Coyote in the many, many Native American languages, is a varied figure and in the Acoma and in the Pueblo tradition Coyote is a funny character. He's shrewd sometimes but he is also a kind of fool at times. He's too smart for his own good, and stuff like that. I think that he doesn't fit easily into a single category. One of those categories—there are a lot—is survival, the resistance in the struggle against colonialism. I know that for Acoma and other Pueblo Indian people, Coyote, or Perruh, is a part of a tradition of literature of resistance, of struggling against what will overcome you, that is, Western colonialism. For example, Tshuushki, or Coyote, is interchangeable with Perruh—*perro* is Spanish for "dog." In some stories Perruh is a figure who represents Indian people in their struggle against the Spanish *soudarrhu*, or the soldier, the Spanish troops who came among the people aggressively, destroying. Perruh is the spokesperson; he outthinks, outsmarts, the foolish soldiers; in that case he is a survivor. He's a figure important in a genre that can be called resistance literature. In a sense because Coyote in some other traditions—for example, in the Northern Californian traditions—is a shaper, or a maker even, and by his wits and intelligence and creative nature, he overcomes odds or sets an example or is a teacher or comes to have people realize something about themselves, obviously, he is going to be a means of speaking for survival.

LC   You describe the English language as a very definite one, "useful in defining things," which in other words means also "setting limits." "But language is not definition . . . language is all-expansive." Language, then, "as perception and expression of experience."[2] Does it go back to your people's use of language?

ORTIZ   I guess all my perceptions and expressions do go back to what

I was born into and what I was developed through, that is, the original experience. That is really what I know. That is, that I was born of the Acoma people, and that my name comes from them. My mother and my father were the most immediate teachers. The elders of my clan were the stuff of life, so to speak, in every way, personal and social. My formation with regards to language was the *dzehni niyah* of the Acoma people: "the way they spoke," the way they thought and felt, the way they perceived. So the writing cannot help but be fundamental. I can only be who I am as an Acoma person. I cannot be anything else. *Tzah dze guwaah ihskah nudahsqkunuuh*, "I cannot be anything else." The language I use is English. Nevertheless, my English language use is founded on the original and basic knowledge of myself as an Acoma person. I cannot be anything except an Acoma man in nature, philosophy, and outlook and so forth. Although, obviously, in terms of technical linguistics, there are going to be influences and implications from other sources. There may be colorings that are not so easily interchangeable and are not synonymous from one language to another. But my frame of reference, being Acoma originally, determines what and how I write today. Even if I did not write anything about Acoma, even if I did not write anything about Native America, I would still have that prior knowledge. Unless I was just totally brainwashed, which is not very far from possibility; I mean, Indian people have changed, but I think consciously and conscientiously they refer to what is fundamental. *Acquumch sthudhah*, "I could not be anything else." As long as I believe that I cannot be anything else, then whatever I say—I may write about MX missiles or about Italy or I may live in Italy—cannot be anything else; I couldn't fail to use language according to my original identity.

LC   In [Kenneth] Rosen's anthology, *The Man to Send Rain Clouds*, you said that language is a way of life, which in my opinion is one of the most beautiful definitions of language.

ORTIZ   It's true, and I have sort of refined that in a way, to mean that by language we create knowledge. Our language is the way we create the world. And I don't mean just spoken language or heard language, but language as the oral tradition, in all its aspects, qualities, and dimensions. Scott Momaday, in his essay "The

Man Made of Words," talks about this particular magic process of language.[3] The process being the act of language; man exists because of language, consciousness comes about through language, or the world comes about through language. Life—language. Language is life, then.

LC What are the contemporary oral stories about among Indians, among Pueblos?

ORTIZ A lot of them are historical. I could not really classify them readily, but I know a lot of them are historical, historical in the sense of recent history. My father would speak of when he was a boy, running away from Indian school, rebelling against changes in the Indian way of life, trying to express certain views about how important it was for him and for the people to retain their heritage. People speak about recent changes, the construction of the railroads and what effect that has had on language, on culture, on the land base, and so forth. The struggle of being Indian, I think, a lot of stories turn on that. The struggle of how and why it is important to be Indian in order to retain one's heritage and identity. A lot of recent oral-tradition stories are based on that. An older category is those stories that continue from way back, from time immemorial, before time, before anything was created, and people come to know themselves through unknown epochs and come into this time. Those stories are obviously very, very important, prehistorically. But they are not only prehistorical, because they speak very relevantly and clearly to the immediate conditions and immediate concerns of people today.

LC So there is always a strong link between past and present.

ORTIZ Oh, yes. There is a real link also between historical stories, recent historical stories, and those other, older stories from the tradition that are in the past but are still very useful now. A lot of the stories that we hear about people—personality profiles—have a lot to do with histories, but they often refer to certain values that Indian people hold precious and dear. Whether the stories are tragic or happy, they are examples of values Indian people should follow, or see as reflections. But stories are very useful. In writing, the stories from both of these categories have current use and current life, they are utilized as contemporary stories, some of which are plots and characters for novels, such as *Love Medicine*, by Louise Erdrich, or Leslie Silko's *Ceremony*. Leslie Silko's novel uses both.

LC   You have said that before the late sixties, there was no tradition of a Native American literature. You did not know yourself of any Native American writers until 1966, but some of the contemporary Native American writers do not accept the word "renaissance." What's your opinion about that?

ORTIZ I have said a couple of times that there was really no Native American literature before the 1960s, which is true with some qualifications. For example, there were writings by Luther Standing Bear; an amount of material from the Bureau of American Ethnology; *Sun Chief*, by Don Talayesva; and there was Alexander Posey writing in English. There was also a tradition of Spanish-language writers, Latin American native writers from Peru, Chile, and Mexico. Some were known in the nineteenth and eighteenth centuries, even as early as that, as chroniclers, poets, scholars; but in English there wasn't a whole lot. Until the 1960s and the third-world literature movement, there was not a large amount of contemporary publications. N. Scott Momaday, Vine Deloria, Jr., and James Welch were the first three contemporary writers in the mid-1960s. Even though twenty or thirty years before, D'Arcy McNickle had published, as Carlos Montezuma, and Charles Eastman had published an autobiography and some fiction and poetry. With James Welch and N. Scott Momaday in 1966–69, Vine Deloria, Jr., with his political, social commentary, and scholarly articles, Native American literature came to be much more prominent. As far as "renaissance" is concerned, I hedge against that word simply because it's a very limited view of what Native American literature is. The reason I said "with some qualifications" is because of that fact. There's the continuing oral tradition which is fundamental to everything, really to everything, whether it's scholarly writing, or poetry or art, or any expressive and perceptive form of human art and endeavor. In that sense the literature has always been there; it just hasn't been written with its more contemporary qualities and motives, nor has it been published. To express certain political and cultural Native American positions, to define and identify more closely the truth, to squash the stereotypes and replace them with the real thing—that effort is contemporary.

The 1960s was very inspirational. It was very creative. It was invigorating. It has a worldwide phenomenon of third-world peoples decolonizing themselves and expressing their indigenous spirit, especially in Africa and the Americas. The process of decolonization includes a process of producing literature. Out of that process of decolonization has sprung a very rich body of literature, but this literature still goes back, in any case, to the beginning of time. "Renaissance" does not really have application—it's misapplied. Oftentimes it's used by critics, book advertisers, publishers' public relations, for their own purposes rather than for the purposes of Native American people. Native American people insist that indeed the colonial experience did suppress the Native American voice, so that by writing there is not so much a renaissance but very much an insistence to put our language, our work, our art, in its rightful place.

LC Do you see the writer's work as a means, in Geary Hobson's words, "to serve the people as well as yourselves"?[4]

ORTIZ Essentially. It has to be. There's no other purpose for which a person lives. Again, I refer to what my heritage is. It's a central philosophy: you don't speak, you don't live except on behalf of your people. You can't live, you are not alone; only because of the people are you in existence. It doesn't just mean people as physical people, but people in terms of people and place, people and their religion, people as the source of who you are. Without that, you are not really anything. So your voice is their voice in a sense, in terms of a collective communal spirit. Obviously, there is a contradiction, as there is in most everything. A person as a spokesperson, a person as an artist who has an ability, a gift given to him by his creator, by the All-Spirit, given to him to utilize, is going to do a lot of his work individually, but with the understanding that he doesn't exist without this context; without this wholeness and source he is nothing. That is essential. Writing is the utilization of this language, the expression of that source of heritage, of identity.

Simon Ortiz

LC   In the past two decades quite a number of scholars have devoted many articles to ethnopoetics. The whole concept of ethnopoetics raises some questions and what we call "counteressay" such as "The Rise of the White Shaman as a New Version of Cultural Imperialism," by Geary Hobson; "An Old-Time Attack Conducted in Two Parts," by Leslie Silko; "Just What's All This Fuss about Whiteshamanism Anyway," by Wendy Rose.[5] What are your concerns in regard to these endeavors?

ORTIZ   In a way, I don't pay attention to them. Ethnopoetics as an endeavor of some scholarship and some art is useful, but what the argument really is, is an argument against exploitation. It's not the field of ethnopoetics itself. I mean, if people who are indigenous to a culture want to approach the subject and try to do a fruitful, productive work in that field, they are welcome to it; a lot of work has to be done, a lot of contemporary Native American literature is within this field of ethnopoetics. But it is the exploitation itself that is the issue. My own outlook on that is—I'm antiexploitation, obviously—this process of colonialism, that is, usurping the indigenous power of the people, taking their land and resources and language and heritage away—that has to be struggled against. We cannot ignore that. You just can't. You have to fight it, to keep what you have, what you are, because they are trying to steal your soul, your spirit, as well as your land, your children, and so forth. The issue of exploitation is of central concern to all Native American people. The writers that we have, I think, are dealing with it in whatever way they can. I think Leslie Silko's *Ceremony* is a very good novel about exploitation, especially through cultural change, or *House Made of Dawn* and *Love Medicine*. There are a number of people who are utilizing indigenous cultures, not just Native American cultures but African cultures. They use themes or characters, Coyote, or Native American images which have particular reference to philosophical and religious ceremonies which are very visual and so easily used, and oftentimes wrongly. And if it's wrong, it's probably exploitative. So the issue for me is exploitation. And there has to be waged a struggle, and a very serious concern about misinformation and exploitation; exploitation means discrimination, racism, and domination over subject people, subject culture, and language. In those terms, which are clear enough, standing against misuse is justified.

Related to this is something that takes place that is diversionary. People have real concerns about their land, about their economic livelihood—where their next meal is coming from, how they are being educated, what their job is going to be, what their cultural integrity is and how intact it is. It is diversionary in the sense that some of these themes and symbols and images and characters like Coyote are often taken into the media context and used to divert. It's a media coup. Those symbols are taken and are popularized, diverting attention from real issues about land and resources and Indian people's working hours. The real struggle is really what should be prominent, but no, it's much easier to talk about drums and feathers and ceremonies and those sort of things. "Real Indians," but "real Indians" only in quotes, as stereotypes and "interesting" exotica.

So it's a rip-off and, of course, Indian writers are not immune from doing some of the same things non-Indian writers do—maybe they do it less, or maybe they are more excused when they do it. There is a real danger in that as well: writing only what is expected of you because you are an Indian. I don't think that's a healthy sign of a growing person or a growing people.

LC   In your poems there are recurring words such as "compassion" and "love." Actually, despite the picture of the Native American faced with annihilation and exploitation, you say the tone of your work is hopeful and optimistic.

ORTIZ   I think someone else actually said that too—I agree. It's hopeful and optimistic, though obviously I'm not writing only of pretty subjects. It's hopeful and optimistic in the sense that struggle is always hopeful and optimistic. As long as people do not stop struggling, they do not become cynical; they may get pessimistic sometimes, but not cynical or hopeless. Compassion and love, simply again, has reference back to *imih ih amoo uh haatse eh hanoh,* "compassion and love for land, for people, for all things." It's a principle of human nature, particularly of Native American people, to love and have compassion.

And so in that sense although there may be tremendous difficulties—annihilation, genocide, when times have seemed to be hopeless—because of that principle of compassion and love, *imih ih amoo uh haatse eh hanoh,* the outlook cannot be anything except hopeful and optimistic. It may be true that you don't have a job, that American capitalism is stealing the ground from under your feet, but as long as there's that love and compassion, you are going to keep struggling and fighting in the courts, trying to choose the right leadership for your own people, trying to find the right words for your people. You're trying to think the clear and necessary things in your counsel with young people, in realizing what your life is to be. That struggle itself, based on compassion and love, is hopeful and optimistic. Look down into Latin America today, in Guatemala, in Chile, in Peru; Indian people there, because of love and compassion, are fighting for their children and their land, in arms. Look here to the Black Hills in South Dakota; people are fighting in whatever way they can, sometimes in small organized movements, sometimes in the courts, trying to get a bill passed through Congress, sometimes in extreme cases in some physical, radical action. As long as there is that love and compassion the outlook has to be hopeful and optimistic.

LC   What do you think of the American studies centers in American universities?

ORTIZ   When they were first established it was a necessary response to the third world's struggle in the United States. I mean the Chicanos, the Puerto Ricans, the blacks, and the Indians were saying, we are no longer going to take a back seat. We'll burn you down, or occupy the president's office. That came from the civil rights movement and the general struggle of colonized people worldwide. The response to this by the universities was to set up Native American studies and other ethnic studies. They were set up rather haphazardly—I suppose in some cases very sincerely, with a sincere wish to have Native Americans and other ethnic peoples part of the university and college system.

In other cases, they were half-serious token gestures. They started out with an office in a back room. Some of them have continued. The universities and colleges are not entirely serious and have cut back, in many cases, Native American instructors who were hired; they have been let go simply because the university still is a part of the larger social and political system; the white system is the authority. In state legislatures you find no Indian people where there are large Indian populations; there are Indian people all over the United States. You still find that the state legislatures, unless they are forced to, are not responding in any real way in terms of having budgets for Native American studies. They are included in the whole pot of the university-college system. The struggle for these ethnic studies, particularly Native American studies programs, has been waged heroically, I think.

The big programs are at the University of Minnesota, University of Oklahoma, UCLA, and Berkeley. The University of New Mexico has a big program, but it's token to a large extent. The University of Arizona and I think Oregon, Washington, and a few others, have Native American studies in place, but I think they are not serious, still. A lot of the programs are just programs; they are not departments, not like the economics department or the history department. Yet they are just as essential to public education, public higher education in the United States, as American history. Native American history is as important and should be considered as important as u.s. history. Yet in hardly any u.s. university are Native American studies given this kind of credence. They are not considered as successful or as prestigious.

Whatever kind of program or department is in place, we have to struggle for. We have to insist that they be there, although they are not there in the way that they should be. But we're holding on. It's just like other issues around the country. We would like people to understand them for what they are, that the land-rights struggle for the Black Hills or for the Hopi and Navajo land in Arizona are important simply because they are important for the nation as a whole. And that Native American studies are important because they are important for the nation as a whole.

LC   What do you think of the non-Indian critics of your work and of American Indian literature in general?

ORTIZ   I haven't read a whole lot of critical works of my own works.

There have been a number of them. The works that I have read, have, unfortunately—I would say 90 percent—a limited perspective, a limited view of my poetry. By that I mean that too often their understanding of my poetry is based on their acceptance and judgment of what a Native American should write about. He should write about Native American settings, he should use images that are Native American, and should use the language and values of that; otherwise he is not acceptable. It is very stereotypical as well as racist, unfortunately, which is perhaps the main concern that I have: critics who don't want to really understand Native American people, that the Native American writer comes from his people. If a critic doesn't understand that people and that land, then he's not going to be able to discuss seriously or with any comprehension what the writer is writing about.

Another point—I guess of criticism of the critics—that I have, is that they write very much from their own education in Western literature. This again is another limitation. You can't discuss the poetics of Simon Ortiz in terms of the poetics of Charles Olson. I remember a discussion, I forget who it was, by some writer from Minnesota at the University of Indiana—he was trying to discuss my writing in terms of what he perceived to be the writing of Charles Olson, writing which comes from two different contexts. It was my book *From Sand Creek*. Our poetics obviously are different. So you can't do that. But unfortunately that is what happens in discussing works by Native American writers by non-Native American or non-Indian critics.

Thirdly, I think that there is a real hesitation, and perhaps even an impossibility, a lack of willingness to accept the Native American people and all that we stand for in America. Because if they really looked at the Native American writer, and that means looking at the Native American people, and that writer's work, the critics would have to look at the underpinning, the structure of their own country, at their own conscience. I think there is a great fear. If the critic really looked at what Native America was and is today, he would have to undo the construct that America according to Western civilization and its rationalizations is. He would have to throw it all out. He would have to say this is all wrong; the Native American is indeed right. There is a real—not only a hesitation—denial of what the real America is; and the real America is the Native America of indigenous people and the indigenous principle they represent. That's the real America. The critics refuse to live with that. It's too fearful. They have to undo what they have learned. They have to admit that their perceptions have been wrong all along. And that's real fearful. Non-Indian historians are about the most guilty in their conception of Native American people. They still rely to such a large extent on the idea that the America that is, is what has been built by Western civilization. They refuse to accept America as Native America. They still are fearful of what America means in terms of today's Indians. If the critic looked at Native American writing, then he would have to admit certain human rights are due Native American people. He would have to say, yes, and agree and press the Supreme Court and U.S. Congress to give the Black Hills back to the Lakota people. He would have to say, yes, the Native American people do own Arizona. Fear is the real hindrance to criticism. It's not going to be just or rational unless self-directed questions are asked by the critics. And not just to look at the work itself but at what the work represents.

LC   Do you see any changes that have taken place in your work?

ORTIZ   My work is more than just my writing. I write about universal things. What else could I write about? I am a human being. I write about the same things that Robert Browning or Shelley or Shakespeare did, maybe not in the same way. Everything changes all the time. One of my first major publications was *Going for the Rain*, 1976. I wrote a book according to what I knew, in four parts, following thematically how a person's life is structured, from when he is born to when he completes his life.

In my next book, *A Good Journey*, which was reissued recently, I utilized the oral tradition. My first major books were more in keeping with what I knew from the Acoma tradition, living in this experience called America.

My book *Fight Back* was more contemporary, in nature and voice, in that it looked at the working conditions and historical conditions of Native Americans; working in the mines, uranium and coal mines of New Mexico, based somewhat historically in terms of the oral tradition, but portraying a picture of people in their daily struggle to make a living. To look at their lives, at the lives of their children in the social-political milieu of modern-day America. Thematically it wasn't too different, but my approach was somewhat different. I was concentrating on the immediate, yet referring to the Pueblo revolt of 1680; that struggle then is very similar to our struggle now. It is much more pointed politically because the 1970s and 1980s were very much a time of political struggle.

My latest book, *Fightin'*, prose short fiction, is a combination. There's nothing about being Indian in there. Just stories of people. Why shouldn't I write about non-Indians? I don't have to dress anybody in feathers. I would say the majority of stories have some sort of Indian connotation. My point in the book was to indeed have Indian people understood as people, like anybody else. We have daily struggles: we argue among ourselves; we get divorced; we need jobs; we try to go to school. We have happy times and sad times. So there is a change all the time. I'm doing a book right now on Big Mountain. I haven't done a whole lot of work on it yet, but it's continuing. Big Mountain—the land and people are speaking. Big Mountain land and people speak as a voice from within the social and political dynamics of this country.

LC   Could you describe your writing process?

ORTIZ   No, I can't. I mean, I could tell you a few things. I try to keep up the habit, and it is a habit to try to write every day. I try to write in the morning and I try to write in the evening. The process itself is in trying to be conscious of what voices are speaking inside me. I will try to write everything down. I try to urge myself to sit down and write conversations and dialogues that I have with people. I try to remember what people said. I try to put them in a context later when I'm writing.

I think that a writer's inspiration really comes from so many things. I couldn't identify each one. I think about writing a lot, and then, if I can, I sit down and write it out. But I am very conscious of the creative process simply as a way of living. I keep a notebook and a journal.

LC   What writers among the contemporary ones are important to you?

ORTIZ   Raymond Carver, a short-story writer. He's an important writer to me in the prose fiction form. N. Scott Momaday and Leslie Silko are very good models, I think, for anyone to follow. Earlier, Erskine Caldwell has been important to me. Some of the writers I was very impressed by in the fifties and sixties generation: like William Burroughs, [Alan] Ginsberg, Gary Snyder, [Theodore] Roethke, Diane Wakoski—writers that were immediate to my generation and were liberating writers of the Beat Generation. The third-world writers in the sixties, like Ralph Ellison, Amiri Baraka, Ishmael Reed, Ethridge Knight, John Williams, Claude Brown, Lorraine Hansbury, other black writers; Native American writers like Momaday and Silko and D'Arcy McNickle. I guess those are some of the writers I look to. I'm sort of an older generation now I guess, but I'm not that old.

LC   You mentioned earlier one of your works in progress. Do you have any other works in progress so far?

ORTIZ   I always have something in progress. I don't know what they are, what they're called. Right now I am doing one—maybe it's going to be a prairie book. I have a short-story collection in mind that I want to get seriously working on. The Big Mountain book is very important to me mainly because people have been urging me to do it. I have been working on a novel that I haven't really worked on for a year and a half or two years, but one of these days perhaps I'll finish that. I've also been involved in a movie project for which a small collective was organized some years ago out of Santa Fe, New Mexico. It's a movie for which a screenplay was produced based on stories that I did—it's actually a novella. It will become a movie some day.

LC   You edited *Earth Power Coming* (1983), an anthology of short fiction published by the Navajo Community College. Why didn't you include any of your stories?

ORTIZ   Editor's prerogative. What's the real reason? I think that I wanted to not get myself in the way. Being editor was enough, I felt. There was no real reason, except that I felt it was important for other writers to be considered. I wanted certain writers—some writers didn't come across even though I begged them—but I did not include myself. I don't think I was selfish or vain not to include myself. I simply wanted to serve as editor, say a few words at the beginning, and have the book have the impact that

I hoped for, and I think it has had. I've been criticized for leaving my stories out; and I am sensitive to that. Perhaps it may have been a mistake; I admit it. But I love the book. I think it is an important work in fiction.

Wendy Rose

Like most of the authors interviewed in this volume, Wendy Rose is a mixed-blood. Unlike most of the others, she was raised in the city. Both these elements in her background reflect conditions of modern Indians, and in her poetry the "urbanized Indian" and the "mixed-blood" take on a special significance.

Born in 1948 in Oakland, California, of a Hopi father and a Miwok mixed-blood mother, Wendy Rose, a doctoral candidate in anthropology at the University of California, Berkeley, has taught in the Native American Studies Program there and currently teaches at California State College, Fresno, where she lives with her husband.

Very active in various Indian organizations, she is a former editor of the American Indian Quarterly. *Rose has published widely in magazines and anthologies. Her* Lost Copper *(1980), a collection of her poetry, was nominated for the American Book Award. Her most recent publications include* What Happened When the Hopi Hit New York *(1982) and* The Halfbreed Chronicles and Other Poems *(1985).*

Over the years, she has gained a solid reputation as a poet. She is also an accomplished painter. One of her favorite subjects, the centaur, reflects what she calls "my hybrid status . . . like the centaur, I have always felt misunderstood and isolated —whether with Indians or with non-Indians." [1]

We met on September 5, 1985, at her house in Fresno, California. We were joined in the interview by an iridescent snake, a sleepy frog warmed by an electric bulb, and a darting lizard, all of them watching us from their glass shelters.

LC   In *The Third Woman*, you have written, "It is my greatest but
            probably futile hope that someday those of us who are ethnic
            minorities will not be segregated in the literature of America."[2]
            Will you elaborate on that?

ROSE   Well, anywhere in America, if you take a university-level course
            on American history or American literature, particularly in lit-
            erature and the arts, it only has the literature and the arts that are
            produced by Americans of European heritage, even then largely
            Northern European. We are left out of the books. Black people
            are left out; brown people are left out; Indian people are left out.
            So you get the impression, going through the American educa-
            tion system, that the only people here are white people. It's not
            just a cultural matter, but it's a political matter. There is a rea-
            son for a society to be that way, that has the literary capacity
            and the technological capacity that America has; there's no ex-
            cuse for the people being so blind, for the people to be wearing a
            blindfold that way. The only possible reason it could happen is
            because it's not an accident; that it's planned. Somebody is bene-
            fiting by having Americans ignorant about what non-European
            Americans are doing and what they have done; what European
            Americans have done to them. Somebody is benefiting by keep-
            ing people ignorant.

LC   Describing one of your trips, from California to Arizona, you
            write that "a half-breed goes from one half-home to the other."[3]
            Could you talk on your "half-breed" identity?

ROSE   My father is a full-blood Hopi from Arizona. He lives on the
            reservation. My mother is mostly Scots and Irish, but also Mi-
            wok, which is an Indian tribe from the area near Yosemite
            National Park here in California. I've always thought in terms of
            being a half-breed because that is the way that both sides of the
            family treated me. The white part of the family wanted nothing
            to do, not only with me, but they were even angry that at one
            point my mother married a man who was Welsh. Even being
            Welsh was too exotic for their taste.

            The Hopi side of my family is more sympathetic to my situa-
            tion, but our lineage is through the mother, and because of that,
            having a Hopi father means that I have no real legitimate place
            in Hopi society. I am someone who is from that society in a
            biological sense, in what I like to think is a spiritual sense, and

certainly in an emotional sense, but culturally I would have to say I'm pretty urbanized: an urban, Pan-Indian kind of person. I grew up with Indian people from all over the country, all different tribes. Some of them had lived on reservations and some of them had spent their whole lives in the city. I was born in Oakland, which is of course a big city. So there was always the sense of not really being connected enough to any one group. A lot of Indian writers have written about that. I think in fact it was James Welch who put it in one of his novels; at one point the protagonist is asked if being a half-breed meant that he had special insights and special privilege into both groups, and in fact to paraphrase his answer, he said what it actually means is you don't have enough of either group. I can understand that; I know what he means.

LC   Is your most recent book, *The Halfbreed Chronicles and Other Poems*, a new image of the "half-breed"?

ROSE   In *The Halfbreed Chronicles* I come to terms with that half-breededness I was talking about earlier. Half-breed is not just a biological thing. It's not just a matter of having one parent from one race and the other parent from another race, or culture, or religion, or anything of that nature. But rather it's a condition of history, a condition of context, a condition of circumstance. It's a political fact. It's a situation that people who would not normally be thought of as half-breed in a biological sense, might be thought of this way in another sense. For example, some poems that are in *The Halfbreed Chronicles* are addressed to people like Robert Oppenheimer. Nobody would ever look at him in a racial sense as a half-breed person, yet at the same time he was in a context and at a time, and made choices in his life, that for me apply the metaphor of half-breed to him. And when people hear the poems from *The Halfbreed Chronicles*, very often people of all races and of all backgrounds, come up to me afterward and say that they can identify with *The Halfbreed Chronicles*. To me that means it worked, because that's the intention. We are in fact all half-breed in this world today.

LC   *What Happened When the Hopi Hit New York* is a kind of journal of your trips to various states. What's the "Indian invisibility" you talk about?

ROSE   There are two ways to look at that. One way is the invisibility that is imposed on Indian people, and that gets back to talking about the American system of education, in which Indians are deliberately made invisible, in which people can grow up in an area surrounded by Indian people who have maintained their culture, who still practice their religion, who live on federally administrated reservation land, and the non-Indians do not know it. That non-Indian people there can be unaware of that is one form of invisibility. Another form of invisibility is that which is self-imposed by the Indian person: in a context of conflict especially, very often in a confrontational or in an uncomfortable situation, an Indian will turn into a potted plant, if you know what I mean. An Indian person may withdraw and become part of the furniture or part of the wall. That's also another form of invisibility. It's protective coloration, like camouflage. It's a survival trait.

LC   Could you talk about your work as an anthropologist?

ROSE   I told Joe Bruchac when he was asking the same question about that in another interview—I told him I was a spy.[4] He thought I was kidding and he repeated the question, and I repeated, "I am a spy." He laughed and figured, okay, that's all he was going to get. But I don't think he realizes to this day that I literally meant, I am a spy. But not in any cloak-and-dagger kind of way; I'm not out to hurt anthropologists. But the fact is that the only academic department at Berkeley that would deal with my dissertation, which involves Indian literature, is the anthropology department. Comparative literature didn't want to deal with it; the English department didn't want to deal with it, in fact the English department told me that American Indian literature was not part of American literature and therefore did not fit into their department.

LC   You talked in the interview with Carol Hunter about your struggle to protect the burial grounds. You said that you acted as a kind of mediator between AIM [American Indian Movement] and the archaeologists, who didn't accept your training as an anthropologist as valid, since you aligned yourself with AIM.[5]

ROSE   They didn't really believe that an Indian person would have studied archaeology. They didn't take seriously the fact that I had actually trained in it. I spent five years doing that kind of work, partly to experiment with the idea that if Indian people go into it maybe there will be some control. If, for example, you found a human burial in an archaeological site, if there were an Indian archaeologist there it would be handled differently. People wouldn't just bring up the remains, and so on. It didn't work; I realized after being there for years that archaeologists are just as capable of lying to Indian people as anyone else. There were some very ugly situations where archaeologists were calling up Indian activists and making threats on their lives at one point, in the Bay area, in San Francisco, in Marin County, in particular. When I talk about protecting the burial grounds, it is both a literal fact and a metaphor. The metaphor is to protect Indian people through, in some instances, trying to neutralize the very weapons that are being used against Indians, by mastering those weapons and then in a sense breaking them from within. It is also a literal fact in the poem by that name, "Protecting the Burial Grounds." That poem was in fact written in front of a bulldozer, on top of an Indian cemetery, where we were sitting to prevent the bulldozer from just going through and ripping up the Indian graves. The mayor of San Jose, which is the city this occurred in, actually called out a SWAT team, which is the Special Weapons and Tactical squad, the people with the big guns, who wear the army-type uniforms and are associated with the city police departments. They all came out and they had been told that there was an Indian riot, that AIM was rioting out there in the cemetery. So they came with their MI6s or MI5s or whatever, those big rifles—they came running out past where we were. They were looking for the riot. We were the riot and we were just sitting there. So then finally they left, and we succeeded. We did manage to save that burial ground. It was in fact preserved.

LC   Does it happen very often?

ROSE   Unfortunately, it doesn't. Unfortunately we usually don't find out that a burial ground has been desecrated until after the fact, because developers know that if the Indian people are in an area, and non-Indian people who sympathize with these concerns know that a burial ground is to be dug up or something like that, they will protest. So they go in, in the middle of the night, and the next morning everybody gets up and it's already done.

LC   Speaking about the "system," graduate schools, academia, do you feel that "there is a line which cultures do not cross," and that every day "you are bumping into that line," as you once said? Is there any way to bridge that gap? Can you see the mixed-blood as a mediator between two cultures?

ROSE   I think there is a way. Certainly individuals can cross the line, or can live on the line. I guess what happens is they live on the line, rather than trying to cross from one into another culture territory. When I said that, I was feeling betrayed because of friendships that I had for many years with a number of non-Indian people; all of a sudden the fact of my being Indian became too much for them to bear, and suddenly it just became a big issue with them. And similarly with Arthur, my husband, who is Japanese-American, same thing. His being Japanese-American suddenly became too much for them and they began acting in a racist way toward us, and we thought they were our friends. And it happened that that quotation was about that time, and we were both feeling pretty bitter about what had happened at that point. Sometimes I do feel pretty pessimistic about it like that, but I also think that even though nobody can ever completely cross over into another person's culture, no matter how big a barrier there seems to be or how different the cultures seem to be, there is a way that some people can transcend that, just as human beings—as long as they don't try to ignore the fact of the culture, as long as they respect the fact that those cultures are different and that they're there and that they're important, that they are important parts of the identities of both those people, no matter how different they are. If they can meet on that ground, then I think there is a way to cross that barrier.

LC   You are a poet and an accomplished painter as well. Is there a kind of interrelated technique between the two media that you use in your poetry and in your painting?

ROSE   It feels the same doing them. It feels the same way inside—to do a painting as to write a poem. It feels like the same impulse. The main difference is, and I don't know how to explain this, the main difference is that with poetry I feel like I am tough enough to take the criticism, but if someone doesn't like my paintings, I just fall to pieces. I'm more professional about poetry, and less so about the paintings I think.

LC American Indian writers and publishing—you have written an article on that and about the difficulty in locating Native American literature in bookshops, which, by the way, is also my own frustrating experience. It's shelved under "Anthropology," and as you said this segregation is not only philosophical but economic, not to say political. Quoting Vine Deloria, as you did in the *Coyote Was Here* interview, "the fact is that the interest in American Indians is a fad that comes around every twenty years."[6] Actually, in 1969, Momaday's *House Made of Dawn* won the Pulitzer Prize. In 1985, *Love Medicine*, by Louise Erdrich, won the National Book Critic's Circle Award—and deservedly so. Of course, in between, scholars and writers have been recipients of awards and fellowships, but I am just speaking about awards which can appeal to a more general and wider audience. Can you see any significant, important change having taken place in the past few years?

ROSE As you can see, *House Made of Dawn* and *Love Medicine* are approximately twenty years apart. The way a lot of us are looking at it now, Louise has it now, we have to wait another twenty years. And she deserves it; both Scott Momaday and Louise Erdrich certainly are accomplished writers who deserve it. But so is Leslie Silko, so is James Welch, but their timing was wrong. They came in between fads.

LC Considering the importance of women in many Indian societies, is feminism synonymous with heritage for American Indian women?

ROSE I would say not. There are a lot of Indian women, myself included, who consider ourselves to be feminist, but we're not feminist like non-Indian women are. We come from a different base; we have a different history. If I'm on the Hopi reservation I am not a feminist; if I'm in Fresno, California, I'm a feminist.

LC Native Americans come from different tribal and cultural backgrounds. Do you see, then, Native American literature as multiethnic as a result of this?

ROSE It is of course in fact a multiethnic literature. And there are certain tribal differences that scholars could pick out if they applied themselves to it. The further back you go the more evident this is. If you go back to the 1930s, for instance, you can see very profound differences between what a Pueblo person would be writing and what someone who is Sioux would be writing. It's not very new of course to have all this published literature by American Indian people around. It's not a brand new thing; it didn't just suddenly pop up with Scott Momaday. The Pan-Indian part of it, where it is not exactly a multiethnic literature, is in the fact that—and this is speculation on my part; I guess this is part of what I am looking at in my own doctoral dissertation—most of the people that I perceive who become writers and who are thinking in terms of actually publishing, and thinking of themselves as writers in the European sense of a writer and a published work, are people who are in that Pan-Indian world. They are people who are familiar with Indian people from various tribes. Now there are some exceptions. Simon Ortiz is an exception. He has a distinctly Pueblo background, but as an adult has become Pan-Indian, has traveled around. In fact, he's addressed that fact in some of his poems—Indians are everywhere. Ray Young Bear is very decidedly of one particular tribal area and in fact has even expressed the feeling that he does not want to deal with Indian people from other tribes, because he is concerned with people of Mesquakie heritage. He considers his work to be an outgrowth of the Mesquakie heritage, and to have nothing really to do with what the rest of us are doing. So there are exceptions. But I think most Indian writers probably are more similar to each other than they are to other members of their tribe who are not writers. I think, for example, culturally I bear more similarity to someone like Maurice Kenny, a Mohawk from New York City, or to James Welch for that matter, who of course is Blackfeet and Gros Ventre, than I do to other Hopi women of my same age who are on the reservation. I have more similarities with those other writers than with other Hopi or Miwok people.

LC   Do American Indian writers have a large audience among Indian people?

ROSE   Increasingly so. The Indian communities are beginning again to value those people who specialize in working with words. That of course was a traditional value at one time. And as Indian people went to the boarding schools and were forced to speak foreign languages and to worship foreign gods and so on, they also lost contact with their own traditions involving the spoken or the written word. I think that's being rediscovered. Increasingly, I find, for example, that I probably give more poetry readings as parts of powwows and tribal functions, grass-roots kind of functions, nonliterary functions, for Indian people in a community now than I do for literary people. And I like that. I enjoy giving poetry readings of course to literary people, too, and to urban audiences and so on. But the feeling of being appreciated by that grass-roots community is also very important to me. I think probably more important than the prestige or academic part of it. And this is something that's very important, I think —things like having poets and novelists as keynote speakers at what had one time been strictly political and social functions— at political rallies, at tribal chairmen banquets. At things of this nature, which used to be completely nonliterary.

LC   Does literature develop a sense of Pan-Indianness?

ROSE   Possibly, yes. But it should be also made really clear that to be Pan-Indian is not to become less tribal. To be tribal and to be Pan-Indian exist side by side, and in fact Pan-Indianism is intended to protect those tribal identities, not to replace them. So there is the Pan-Indian aspect to the literature, but with much of the same excitement generated by the literature that is in the English language in the form of the novel, or poetry. We then turn around in our own communities and can print things like booklets for children of traditional stories; we can print things like language primers in our own native languages, much of it with the impetus that originally came from writing the poetry and the novels.

LC   In American universities there is an increasing number of American Indian studies centers. What do you think of them?

ROSE   Well, I teach in one. It's not in a university, but I have taught in universities. I'm now at a city college, a two-year college. But I have taught at the University of California at Berkeley, and I have taught at California State University here in Fresno, in both instances in Native American studies, and now at Fresno City College. I see it as something that at the moment is very necessary, as part of the ethnic studies experience. It's something that's been left out of the curriculum, is still left out of the curriculum, unless we go there and put it in. And the only way we can go there and put it in is to concentrate on just those things. And if Indians are left out of every other class on the university campus, even where they are pertinent—for example, leaving Scott Momaday out of a class on twentieth-century American literature, something like that—somewhere else there has to be a balance. There has to be someone somewhere else who is going to emphasize Scott Momaday to the exclusion of the ones who are emphasized in the other class. I hope that at some point that will become balanced. I hope that pretty soon an American literature class will just automatically include someone like Scott Momaday—and some of the other people: Charles Eastman, you know, the other writers in our history.

I also hope that there will continue to be some kind of program where Indian people will be doing the teaching. If courses in Native American studies were to go into the so-called mainstream departments, if Native American history were just taught through the history department, it would not be an Indian person teaching it. Even if they taught from the same cultural and political viewpoint, it would probably not be an Indian teacher. So part of what we are doing in these ethnic-studies departments is building up a core of professional academic people, a core of professional scholars.

LC   What's the response you get from your students?

ROSE   Well, it ranges—I have very large classes for Native American studies. Up at Berkeley you're likely to have a class with ten people in it, but down here it's more likely to be fifty. It varies. At the two-year college I find that students are much more receptive to the Native American studies than they were at the four-year university in the same city, here in Fresno. At the four-year university I had students who were calling me a squaw in class. I had students who, as I'd be walking across campus, would yell rude things at me that would be racist in nature; I was told not to talk about political controversy. They are among the reasons why I left the university, and I went to the city college here. Where I am now, some of the students have difficulties with the material primarily because they were brought up with a very narrow focus: if it isn't in the Bible it can't be true. That is the major problem, which is not as much a problem as just plain hostility.

LC   What do you think of non-Indian critics and readers of your work?

ROSE   When non-Indian critics, generally speaking, criticize my work, I find it useful. The critics that bother me are the ones who set out to review my work or the work of some other Indian writer and state at the beginning of the review that they can't really do it justice because they haven't taken enough anthropology. They drive me bats, because when I write my books of poetry, they are in the English language. When I use Hopi or other Native American terms, or Japanese terms, terms that are not in English, I explain them. I use a footnote as a courtesy, with the assumption that most of the readers of my work will be reading it in English. So with that assumption I use footnotes. I wish that the academic poets I might be reading would have the same courtesy for me to explain some of the culture-specific terms that they use. But they don't.

LC   In Geary Hobson's words the "white shaman" is a writer who in his poems assumes the persona of a shaman, usually in the guise of an American Indian medicine man.[7] Would you like to add a few remarks on that?

ROSE   A few remarks. The term was coined by Geary Hobson. These are not just people who take on the persona of the shaman in their poetry but are people who actually even outside the realm of poetry take on a fabricated persona. The problem is one of integrity, very simply. I have no difficulty with people taking on an Indian persona and trying to imagine through their work what it would be like, for example, to be at the Wounded Knee massacre, or to be a man or a woman in Indian society. Fine. As long as it's really clear that that's what it is—an act of imagination. In my own work, if I put myself into the shoes of Robert Oppenheimer, it clearly is an act of imagination. I'm not going to pretend to people that I'm Robert Oppenheimer, or that I have some special insight into Robert Oppenheimer's mind. I'm going to imagine something about Robert Oppenheimer and I'm going to express the imagination. It's not an expression of him; it's an expression of me. If people who want to write about Native American spirituality or any of those kinds of issues were to simply start it out by saying something like: this is an act of my imagination; this is something I have been thinking about; this is something I feel; this is how I see it. Fine. But what happens is, that we get people, and this is who we call white shamans, people who say they have some special gift to be able to really see how Indians think, how Indians feel; that when they do it, it's real. One of them even had the audacity one time to tell me that I could not write poems; in the particular instance it was a poem about Tsu'hsi, the empress dowager of China; he told me I shouldn't write a poem about her because how could I understand the Chinese culture, but then he said it would be okay for him to do it because it was easier for someone who was white to put themselves into the shoes of other cultures, than it would be for other people.

LC   Can you see any evolution in your work?

ROSE   I hope it's getting better. I don't know. It isn't really my job to try to analyze my own work. I'm more comfortable analyzing someone else's work. But I try to improve. I hope that, like anyone else regardless of what they're doing, I hope that as I grow the work grows. I hope I am growing; I hope the work is growing.

LC   Could you describe your writing process?

ROSE   Well, I explained it one time, on radio, as the sensation of being sick in your stomach, in that you suddenly have to throw up, suddenly, you have to vomit. There is no way you can stop it. It has to happen. It's a bodily process in which the material is expelling itself from your body. That's what it feels like to me in a mental or emotional way. Suddenly it's there and it has to be expelled. It's going to come out whether I want it to or not. If I don't have something to write on, it comes out of my mouth. It's got to come out one way or another.

LC   Could you talk about your works in progress?

ROSE   There's one book that is primarily political work, which is looking back over the Indian movement for the twenty-five or so years that I've been involved with it, which is going to be called "Going to War with All My Relations." I don't have a publisher for it yet, so there will be probably something worked out about it pretty soon. There's one book I have in mind that he [her husband] doesn't want me to do. That's called, "How Come Arthur Isn't a Cowboy?" A couple of things like that are in progress.

Leslie Marmon Silko

Leslie Marmon Silko was born in Albuquerque in 1948. Of mixed ancestry—Laguna, Mexican, and white—she grew up at the Pueblo of Laguna, not far from the Los Alamos uranium mines and Trinity Site, where on July 16, 1945, the first atomic bomb was detonated.

From earliest childhood she was familiar with the rich cultural lore of the Laguna and Keres people through the stories told by her grandmother Lillie and "Aunt Susie" (her grandmother Hank Marmon's sister-in-law). Both women had a deep influence on Silko, passing down to her "an entire culture by word of mouth."[1]

She attended a Catholic school, commuting to Albuquerque, and in 1969 she received a bachelor's degree in English from the University of New Mexico. In her college years she wrote a short story, "The Man to Send Rain Clouds," based on a real incident that happened at Laguna. The story was published in 1969, and she was rewarded with a National Endowment for the Humanities Discovery Grant. She enrolled for three semesters in the American Indian Law Program at the University of New Mexico, but she rejected a legal career for writing. In 1974 she published a book of poetry, Laguna Woman. *That same year, seven of her stories appeared in one of the first anthologies on contemporary Native American writing,* The Man to Send Rain Clouds, *edited by Kenneth Rosen. Later she taught at Navajo Community College at Tsaile, Arizona, and then went to Ketchikan, Alaska, where she wrote her first novel,* Ceremony

(1977), which received enthusiastic praise both from critics and readers. In the past few years Silko has taught at the University of New Mexico and at the University of Arizona. She has two sons and currently lives in Tucson.

Her short stories have been included in Best Stories of 1975 *(1976) and* Two Hundred Years of Great American Short Stories *(1976). In recent years she has been awarded a National Endowment for the Arts Fellowship and a MacArthur Foundation grant to complete her novel,* The Almanac of the Dead.

Owing to this work in progress, she announced, "no more travel for lectures, readings or conferences, and no more interviews over the telephone, in person, or by mail." But in spite of her declaration, when I called her from downtown Tucson, she agreed to a meeting at her home on September 26, 1985.

Leslie's house was on a mountain covered with saguaro stylized shapes. A few horses stood in a little corral at its side, and two dogs bearing marks from coyote bites barked furiously at my arrival. Newspapers were stuffed under the back door to keep out snakes, although Leslie soon proudly introduced me to a small, exotic serpent. The interview took place in a room filled with purple light, huge Indian masks, pueblo pottery, and Leslie's art of storytelling.

A NOTE FROM LESLIE MARMON SILKO

When my friend Professor Laura Coltelli sent the transcription of our interview I was horrified at how crude and convoluted and wild my answers and comments about time-space and particle physics looked on the page. I made attempts to edit the transcription of the interview so that I would sound slightly more coherent. But the longer I looked at the interview, the more awkward and unsatisfactory my responses seemed.

Now, months later, suddenly I understand the source of my resistance to this interview: in the process of writing my novel, *Almanac of the Dead*, my subconscious had cannibalized this interview to create an important character, the Mexican Indian woman I call Angelita. I realize now I could not edit or salvage this interview because the character called Angelita had already taken possession of all my notions and ideas about particle physics, space-time, and European thought. The character, Angelita, comes up with wild and strange notions about Europeans, their history and cosmology, but Angelita is funnier and more articulate than I; and Angelita doesn't sound as pompous.

The novel is a voracious feeder upon the psyche; *Almanac of the Dead* has dominated my life since 1981. The following interview has interest and value in so far as it illuminates the evolution of certain characters and themes in *Almanac*. As for interviews in general I think novelists should write more and talk less.

Leslie Marmon Silko
November 23, 1988
Tucson

LC   In *Ceremony*, Thought-Woman thinks and creates a story; you are only the teller of that story. Oral tradition, then: a tribal storyteller, past and present, no linear time but circular time. Would you comment on that?

SILKO   The way I experienced storytelling as a young child, I sensed that people—the person you know or loved, your grandma or uncle or neighbor—as they were telling you the story, you could watch them, and you could see that they were concentrating very intently on something. What I thought they were concentrating on was they were trying to put themselves in that place and dramatize it. So I guess as I wrote those words, Ts'its'tsi'nako, Thought-Woman, and the Spider, I did not exactly mean in the sense of the Muse, at least as I understand the Muse with a capital "M." What was happening was I had lived, grown up around, people who would never say they knew exactly, or could imagine exactly, because that's an extremely prideful assertion; they knew what they felt, but you could try those words and all that follows about Thought-Woman, the Spider, as being a storyteller's most valiant—and probably falling short at the same time—attempt to imagine what a character in a story would be like, and what she would see, and how in the logic of that old belief system, then, things would come into creation.

LC   As is said of some archaic societies, there is a revolt against historical time? What about the concept of time?

SILKO I just grew up with people who followed, or whose world vision was based on a different way of organizing human experience, natural cycles. But I didn't know it, because when you grow up in it, that's just how it is, and then you have to move away and learn. I think that one of the things that most intrigued me in *Ceremony* was time. I was trying to reconcile Western European ideas of linear time—you know, someone's here right now, but when she's gone, she's gone forever, she's vaporized—and the older belief which Aunt Susie talked about, and the old folks talked about, which is: there is a place, a space-time for the older folks. I started to read about space-time in physics and some of the post-Einsteinian works. I've just read these things lately, I should tell you, because in Indian school, in elementary school, I got a very poor background in mathematics and science. So it has only been recently that I've ventured, because I'm so curious. And why am I interested suddenly in the hard, hard, cold, cold (something I thought I would never be) so-called sciences? Because I am most intrigued with how, in many ways, there are many similarities in the effect of the so-called post-Einsteinian view of time and space and the way the old people looked at energy and being and space-time. So now I am doing reading and what I am finding is that if the particular person, the scientist, is a good writer—can write in an expository manner clearly—then I'm finding if I read along doggedly, reading it as you would poetry, not trying to worry if you're following every single line, I'm starting to have a wonderful time reading about different theories of space and distance and time. To me physics and mathematics read like poetry, and I'm learning what I try to tell people from the sciences: you know, don't get upset, don't demand to follow it in a logical step-by-step [fashion]. Just keep reading it. Relax. And that's what I did. I just went with it. I would get little glimmers of wonderful, wonderful points that were being made. I got so excited. I told somebody: "I'm only understanding a fifth of it, because I never had very good mathematics or physics or anything. But, you know, I really like to keep on learning." That's what I'm doing right now. In some ways you would say what I'm reading and thinking about and working on is many light-years away from the old folks I grew up with, and how they looked at time. But not really. Really what I'm doing now is just getting other ideas about it. Although you might not notice it from the books you would see around, I am working on just that right now. And of course this new book I'm working on is also about time, so it's very important to me.

LC   *Ceremony* has a male protagonist, but it is a story created by a woman, told by a woman [but a story] already known by another woman, Tayo's grandmother, whose words conclude the novel. Does it stress women's role and importance in the Pueblo society?

SILKO   Certainly, that's part of it, just because women hold such an important position in temporal matters—the land-title, the house, the lineage of the children; the children belong to the mother's line first, and secondarily of course to the father. There is not any of this peculiar Christian, Puritan segregation of the sexes. So there is very much wholeness there. Women remembering, listening, hearing the things that are said and done. There's no prohibition against a woman repeating a funny story that's basically about the copulation of say, two coyotes, any more than a man. There's no difference, but you do find that in different cultures. Therefore, a girl has as much of a chance, as she grows up, to be a teller, to be a storyteller, as a boy-child. And as we always like to say, the women are tougher and rougher and live longer, so chances are we'll live to tell our version last, because of course we all know that there are different versions. I can say I will outlive so-and-so and then I will tell that story one time when she cannot be around, or later whisper it to somebody. But the viewpoint in the novel wasn't intentional; I mean, I didn't sit down and say, "This is what I'm going to do." About two-thirds of the way through I was pleased for what I knew then; I was pleased with those characters. I'm not really pleased with some of them now, especially the women. I think I understand why they're not as fully realized as the men.

LC   There are three women who play a very important role in the novel: Night Swan, Ts'eh, Betonie's grandmother; all associated with the color blue, the color, by the way, which is associated also with the West, yet their relationship with each other is somehow mysterious, even if Night Swan seems to be an antici- pation of Ts'eh. Is that correct?

SILKO   I am interested in certain convergences and configurations, where many times the real focal point is the time. I'm interested in these things that aren't all linked together in some kind of easy system. For example, the Ute woman, Helen-Jean, appears very briefly. She's in the bar when Rocky's friends, the drunks he hangs around with, Harley and Emo, are there. She is telling her- self, "pretty soon I'm going to go home" and she does try to send money back to this poor, poor reservation. She's just there, and she goes. In one way, if you were judging her by more conven- tional structural elements of a novel, she just sort of comes and goes. But I would rather have you look at her, and get a feeling for her, so that when we make a brief reference to Tayo's mother, the one who dies early and is disgraced and so on, then I don't have to tell you that story. I'm trying to say that basically what happened to Tayo's mother is what happened to Helen-Jean, is what happened to—on and on down the line. These things try to foreshadow, or resonate on each other.

LC   Actually, the Gallup story and the Helen-Jean story at first seem to be separate stories within the main plot. Do you relate them to the story-within-a-story technique of the old storytellers?

SILKO   When I was writing Ceremony, I just had this compulsion to do Helen-Jean. But the other part, about Gallup, is the only surviv- ing part of what I call stillborn novels; and the Gallup section is from one of the stillborns. And you have to remember that when I was writing Ceremony I was twenty-three, maybe twenty-four, years old; I really didn't expect anything to happen. So I figured nothing's going to happen with this anyway, and I really like the Gallup section, and in a strict sense it sort of hangs off like feathers or something. It's tied to it, and it belongs there, but its relationship is different. I put that in for exactly the same reason, vis-à-vis structure, as I did the Helen-Jean part. Again, it was important to see a woman caught somewhere—I wouldn't even say between two cultures—she was just caught in hell, that would be the woman who was Tayo's mother, or the woman who is Helen-Jean, or the woman who was down in the arroyo with the narrator of the Gallup section. And the reason I did this—which in a way only storytellers can get away with, narratives within narratives within narratives—is that [the stories] are in the ultimate control of the narrator. But for me there was something necessary about taking a perspective which pulled me and the listener-reader back always. It's tough to write about humans living under inhuman conditions; it's extremely difficult just to report it; one gets caught up in one's own values, and politics, and so forth. And I think I fear too much a kind of uncontrolled emotion. And so it had to be done like that. But it's the old theme, which the old lady at the end articulates: "Seems like I've heard these stories before."

One of the things that I was taught to do from the time I was a little child was to listen to the story about you personally right now. To take all of that in for what it means right now, and for what it means for the future. But at the same time to appreciate how it fits in with what you did yesterday, last week, maybe ironically, you know, drastically different. And then ultimately I think we make a judgment almost as soon as we store knowledge. A judgment that somehow says, "I've heard stories like that" or "I would tend to judge her harshly except I remember now . . ." All of this happens simultaneously. When I was working on *Ceremony*, these were deliberate breaks with point of view. And I agonized over them, because after all I knew that those kinds of shifts are disturbing. But ultimately the whole novel is a bundle of stories.

LC   In a story there are many stories.

SILKO   Right. You can get away with it. I was aware of that. What caused those first two attempts at the novel to be stillborn was that I had a narrator who was a young woman, about my own age. And it just did not work. It just becomes yourself. And then you have to look at how limited you are, and so the only way you can break out of your personal limitations is to deal with a fictional character. Fictional characters are very wonderful. They are parts of ourselves, but then you get to fix up the parts that don't work so well for you in your mind.

LC   A young man named Tayo is the main character of a legend transcribed by Franz Boas. Is it still a Laguna or Pueblo name?

SILKO   I don't know for sure, but I think it probably is. The sound of it was on my mind. I guess in Spanish, Tayo Dolores is like Theodore, or something, but I didn't even think of that. I just liked the sound of it.

LC   It's a familiar name.

SILKO   It's a familiar sound. When I say I liked the way it sounded, I mean comfortable, intimate, the person you're going to travel with. As a writer you're going to have to follow this character. You'd better really feel comfortable with him.

LC   In "Storyteller" there is an intriguing association concerning the red and the white colors. The color yellow is very often associated with something connected with the whites: "yellow machines"; "yellow stains melted in the snow where men had urinated"; "the yellow stuffing that held off the coat"; "the yellow flame of the oil stove." What's the meaning of all that?

SILKO   First of all, of course, yellow in the Pueblo culture is an important color. It's a color connected with the East, and corn, and corn pollen, and dawn, and Yellow Woman, [the heroine of the abduction myths]. So I don't think we can go too far in a traditional direction, with what yellow means. It's one of my favorite stories, because it's outside of the Southwest. And it's taking myself as a writer, and working with stories, and making radical changes. To tell you the truth, in that particular arctic landscape I suppose to hunters, anywhere except in the town, yellow could be a sign that a herd had freshly been by. In other words, I guess what I'm trying to say is maybe in this particular piece it's fairly insular; how the color works isn't so easily tied to any particular belief system. But certainly up there, just an endless field of white, and that cold pure yellow is kind of an extreme, and when it appears, it's intrusive.

LC   That's the word.

SILKO   And it stops things. The rising of the moon, and the way the stars look up there is wonderful, part of that is the color. And certain colors which you can find in the sky, for example, with the aurora, mean more. The key figure I guess is the field of white, if you want to talk about the field of white like a painter, the blank or whatever. Generally yellow, on that field of white, is, in the winter, abnormal—it's just within that story that yellow works like that. It's very much the context of the northern landscape.

LC   How does the oral tradition go on?

SILKO   By that you mean at Laguna or any given place?

LC   Among Indian people.

SILKO   That's a very difficult question really. One day it dawned on me, I had this sudden recognition that already there were things that I had seen and done, and people that I had been with at home, who had taught me things, that had been gone a long time. What I see is astonishing, on one hand, very exhilarating, and on the other hand very frightening, the rapid change. I was born in 1948; I'm talking about things I saw in 1954 done on the reservation, vis-à-vis the Pueblo people, or maybe some of the Navajo, or even some of the white people that lived on ranches nearby. That part of America, the small rancher, the Pueblo people, the Navajos and the Spanish-speaking land-grant people. It's been such a change, that I would have to be a terrible, pompous liar to sit here and tell you that it's just in my area that I see it. The change in outlook and how the people live in these very distinct racial and cultural communities in New Mexico, and in America, since the middle fifties, is just amazing. It makes me want to laugh at some of the older ethnologists and ethnographers. I would say that most of the material—not most; now I'm starting to use words that are a little too far-spreading—but I think that many of the models that were constructed in the late fifties and early sixties by so-called social scientists, ethnologists, ethnographers, about acculturation, social changes, how humans learn language, how language affects the way you think, and so on, were so incomplete that those models have to be overturned. Not just for Indian people in New Mexico or Arizona, but African tribal people, all of the people who have gone through this period of colonialism. That is, in a sense, what I am concerned with writing about, what I'm working with right now. It goes on.

LC   You said once that we should make English speak for us.

SILKO   At that time it hadn't really occurred to me that people who are born English speakers are trying to make English speak for them too. What I was saying was a little naive. The great struggle is to make whatever language you have really speak for you. But I won't back down from it, in the sense that I like to take something that is a given, a given medium or a given mode, and then treat it as if it were a fantastical contest or trick. Here are the givens; you only have this and this; this is what you are trying to describe; these are the persons you are trying to describe this to; we don't want them to just see it and hear it; we want them to be it and know it. This is language and you deal in it. That's the most intriguing thing of all. And of course all artists to one degree or another, whether it's with sculpture or music or whatever, are working with that. And I stand by that. And there are certain things, for example, when you talk about space-time, and all kinds of little insoluble puzzles about time-space, and how it is that we can use language to define language. We have to use language in order to define language. I'm getting more and more humbled, to the point where I think it's a wonder we can express the most simple desire in our given tongue, clearly. And sometimes I wonder if we can even hope for that.

LC   What's the process by which you move from the oral tradition to the written page? How does it work?

SILKO   It just happens. From the time I could hear and understand language, I have been hearing all these stories, and actually I have been involved in this whole way of seeing what happened—it's some kind of story. But when it finally happened, I wasn't conscious about mixing the two. I was exposed [to stories] before school, and then I went to school and read what you read in America for literature and history and geography and so on. And then at the age of nineteen, I was at the University of New Mexico. And I had just had a baby—Robert, who's now nineteen —and Robert's father, my first husband, said how would you like to take a class where you could get an easy A? And I said, well, I would like that, you know, because having this baby and all, it would be nice to bring up my grade-point average. So I took a creative-writing class. The professor gave us little exercises. Then he said one day, "We want a character sketch," even a character, and I thought, oh no! I had thousands. And so I did it. And then he said, "We want a story." I thought, Is he serious? Is this all it is? I just cashed in on all those things I'd heard.

But a more important, fundamental thing happened, probably in the very beginning, which was in the first grade. I learned to love reading, and love books, and the printed page and therefore was motivated to learn to write. The best thing, I learned, the best thing you can have in life is to have someone tell you a story; they are physically with you, but in lieu of that, since at age five or six you get separated from all of those people who hold you and talk to you, I learned at an early age to find comfort in a book, that a book would talk to me when no one else would. Or a book would say things that would soothe in a way that no person could.

So the fifth grade is when I really started actually writing secretly; but it wasn't until I was nineteen and got to the university, that the two things just fell into place, which was all of my early attitudes and things I'd heard; plus, I'd read Faulkner, I'd read Flannery O'Connor, Henry James, Kate Chopin, Isak Dinesen. And then this guy says, "Write a story." A lot of people were saying, "I don't know what I'm going to write about." And I thought, I don't know what I'm going to start writing about first. And so the two things just kind of crashed together. What I learned from all the years of reading Thomas Hardy and reading *Julius Caesar* were little mundane things, because Shakespeare has all these clowns and these little underlings who have funny little squabbles but have their little moment when they pipe up and say something that makes the bigger story roll around. That experience from reading helped me realize what a rich storehouse I had. And then, I like to get A's, and I like to have people pat me on the head. So I could just do it. But that's how come I could, because I'd had a rich oral tradition for quite a long time; I mean even now if I go home I can hear all these wild stories about what my family's done, and my cousins and stuff. But also I was encouraged to read. I loved books. And when things were rough, when I was in a bad situation, I could read a book. It wasn't conscious, but it just happened in my life.

LC Do you feel that as in the oral tradition, the relationship between the storyteller and his or her audience, must be a dynamic one?

SILKO It would be easier on me, in what I have to do in order to satisfy these urges, if there were a place. I really think that it was wonderful during the time when the storyteller could practice her or his art. I went to China for three weeks; the Chinese Writers Association invited a group of American writers. They showed us this teahouse, and there were these two seats, with little wooden chairs with nice little pillows, and they said every night of the week, except Friday and Sunday or something, storytellers come. People buy their tea from us [the writers] and they sit in there, and these two storytellers sit across from them—sometimes it's two old men and sometimes it's two old women—and the teahouse people. This was in Sh'eie, near where all the terra-cotta warriors were dug up. Anyway, they showed us this room because one of our interpreters said, "Hey look, this is what still goes on in China." And all these people are sitting there listening and drinking their tea. And there's another storyteller there so you can say, "Well, isn't that what you think?" Or you can do routines like, "Oh, you always tell it like that!" I really think that that's wonderful, interacting directly like that, even having another storyteller there who might be trying to catch you on something, which of course means you get to catch them, if you can, with the people there. A wonderful kind of positive energy is generated which you can partake in, and you can get more; I'm not saying I don't get any when I write, or I wouldn't be sitting here a lot. I really think that to me the real, the ultimate moment, is when you have a couple of storytellers and a really engaged, respectful audience. So that I guess in a strange sort of way I'm saying that in Western European culture, the theater, drama, and/or what we have in the United States, mostly it's kind of declined now. The stand-up comedians, someone like Lenny Bruce, that play an older kind of role of the traveling teller or the troubadour, are the storytelling experience.

LC How do you try to achieve it in your works?

SILKO I'm very aware of a physical audience, whether I'm reading at some distant place, or whether I'm sitting with people. I'm so aware of it, that when I sit down at the typewriter, there's only me. I feel the distance dramatically. Do you see what I mean? At Laguna I have an uncle who's very young; he's only ten years older, he's just like a brother, and his wife and his sisters are very brilliant. They've traveled and gone places to school. They've all come back. They have funny ways of saying things; they like to laugh and tell horrifying stories, but the way they tell them is really funny, and you're laughing. But when I'm writing I have to go into that room, I have to go in there alone, and I'm the one who makes me go in there, day after day. And I'm the one that has to put up with the days when it looks really bad—the words that I write. Then in that area I am just doing what I do, and I have no thought of anyone ever reading it, because I can only relate to someone who's sitting there. I really don't consciously think that much about an audience. I'm telling the story, I'm trying to tell it the best way I can, in writing, but I'm not thinking, Maybe we better have him do this, or Maybe we better not have her do that. I don't think that way.

LC Humor is one of the main features of modern American Indian literature, central to the real meaning of the story itself. Is there a difference between the use of humor in the old Indian stories and in the contemporary ones?

SILKO You know I haven't really thought about whether there's a difference. I'm so attuned to seeing the many similarities. Same thing, referring to the same incident, especially areas in justice, loss of land, discrimination, racism, and so on, that there's a way of saying it so people can kind of laugh or smile. I mean, I'm really aware of ways of saying things so you don't offend somebody, so you can keep their interest, so you can keep talking to them. Oftentimes these things are told in a humorous way. Even punning—you know, the people at Laguna have such a delight with language, going back to how the Korean people loved language and words. So that in English they like to make puns, and they know a little Spanish, or a little Navajo, or a little anything. So their sheer delight in such things, that goes on and always has—that's an area where I can't see that there's been any big shift.

LC In an interview in 1976 with Per Seyersted about the American Indian Movement, you said, "It is more effective to write a story like 'Lullaby' than to rant and rave."[2]

SILKO Certainly for me the most effective political statement I could make is in my art work. I believe in subversion rather than straight-out confrontation. I believe in the sands of time, so to speak. Especially in America, when you confront the so-called mainstream, it's very inefficient, and in every way possible destroys you and disarms you. I'm still a believer in subversion. I don't think we're numerous enough, whoever "we" are, to take them by storm.

LC So is it a matter of how to awaken public opinion to Indian problems, or is it just a matter concerning the very nature of the American Indian Movement?

SILKO No, I think it's more a question of how. You know, I understand the tactics, every step of the way. In a way I'm not even critical of anything particularly that the American Indian Movement has done. I'm just saying that with the givens that I have, with what I do best, and sort of where I found myself, that that isn't where I can do the best work. I certainly understand and a lot of times share the anger and bitterness, and the confusion over certain kinds of policies and attitudes. America is strange; it's very strange for Americans to have to confront whatever color you are. You can be a black American, a Native American, or an Asian American. If you're very upper-middle class and extremely comfortable, you can drive through any city or town home from your job, and if you have a brain that halfway works at all, just driving home you will see things. We can drive from where I drove today up here, and you can see where the distribution method is pretty much unfair toward people with lesser opportunities, and so on. If you're a very sensitive person, it can be real disturbing, just to be around at any time. I understand it, though I also understand, maybe in a more practical way, the conservatism, and the kind of respect yet for order and law that Americans have. And I don't care what color they are. It's kind of heartbreaking, in South Africa, some of the interviews with South African blacks and colored people, these old folks who are in their sixties. My heart breaks. I think about them like the old folks that were around at Wounded Knee, and when that stuff was going on. That isn't the kind of world they saw. And some of their children, and almost all of their grandchildren are doing things, saying things, and having things done to them, and I would say that is not a unique or peculiar experience to those little old people in South Africa. You could have gone to Belfast ten years ago; I mean, fill in the blanks. And that moves me, that moves me. Therefore, I was born in the in-between. I understand why the old folks cry, and don't understand why they have to keep burying. You know, I'm in a strange place. And I don't condemn one or the other. I do understand where I am most effective, if you want to call yourself a tool, which I don't really call myself. I'm better off doing what I do. As a terrorist or militant I'd be good for like one suicide raid, and then that'd be the end of me. Now, you know, if you want to use me like that—and I'm not a good spy.

LC   Could you describe your creative process?

SILKO   Well, when I was younger, I figured it was just that certain things that I heard I didn't forget. And then I would have a professor or somebody tell me I had an assignment. So I would just go and I would pull it out, and what I would pull out, of course I would always work on. And sometimes I would just take bits and pieces and make it up, because even when I was a little girl I had sort of a wild imagination. Now I'm beginning to realize that almost everything that happens to me is interesting, and I make notes but I don't really have to make notes. I started just recently though to keep notes and little scribbles here and there, and I do it to laugh at what I thought was important, and what I thought I should remember writing, and then how I feel about it six or eight months later. And what's really, really going to be an important image or theme or character trait stays with me.

And I can remember what some of the old folks said. Years ago these [recording] machines were new, and Dad believed in technology. And he'd go to the old-timers and say, "just go ahead and tell it, and that way if all these kids around here don't remember . . ." And you know, he'd count himself in, "I never listen, better tell it to a machine; you can't trust all of us, we might not remember." And some of the old folks agreed, and did it, archival stuff. But a lot said, "If what I have to say, if my story is really important and has"—they wouldn't say relevance, but that's what it is—"relevance to people, then they'll remember it, and they will say it again, and if it doesn't then it's gone, and it dies out." That's a very harsh point of view, but the older I get, the more I come around to it. And in writing I've discovered that that's how my brain works.

What happened with this novel [*Almanac of the Dead*] now,

around about September 1980, I just started feeling parts and places and characters; it was as if you had shattered a two-hour movie. Some of it didn't have dialogue. Like if you took two hours of a feature film and tore it or chopped it up and mixed it all up. These things started coming to me. I began making notes, and I did other things. I finished *The Arrow Boy and the Witches* movie, and still these things came, and they came and they came. I would do extended work on sections, and finally in the summer of 1983, I figured I'd better start. I'd be with people. We'd be at a restaurant, nice people, people I basically liked, or [I'd be] talking to someone and having a fine conversation, and then I would think of something, and I'd have to start saying, "Oh, excuse me," and then I would scribble a note. And so I knew it was there. It was as if I would see things. I have many, many boxes of newspaper clippings, especially about Central America, Nicaragua, politically the rightwing shift in America. It was as if somewhere else something was going on, and every now and then some would float up to the top. And I'd have to write it down. Then I knew I had to start. By then I even had characters; I didn't have all of them, and I didn't know everything. But it's a very big book and it has very many characters. It literally just imposes itself upon me. I find that it's predictable— predictably, there's certain interest and areas. It has a lot to do with where Tucson is, because the U.S. military is very nervous about instability in Central America, and of course Mexico. The day of the earthquake, the bankers who were so glad to lend them money, the serious American bankers who wanted to make money off those people, found out that the International Monetary Fund said no to Mexico, and then the earthquake came. Anyway, there's a bunch of military generals all along this border, who full-well believe that the economic situation in Central America and Mexico can only get worse, that it will be destabilized; there will be basically a kind of movement to try to shift around. Whether we can dare call it a revolution, I don't want to say. This is the first place and the only place I've lived in six years—but the CIA base for helicopters and training is right over there. That is a part of right now and my life and what's happening right now. And also I find very much has blossomed out in this novel. But my process is mostly, not totally, subconscious, not conscious. The reason I write is to find out what I mean. I know some of the things I mean. I couldn't tell you the best things I know. And I can't know the best things I know until I write.

LC   Could you speak a little bit more of your new novel [*Almanac of the Dead*], still in progress?

SILKO   Well, you know it's about time, and what's called history, and story, and who makes the story, and who remembers. And it's about the Southwest. But this time I have purposely, deliberately, taken Indian characters, one in particular, and I've dumped him off the reservation early. He's an older man, too; he's a man and he retired. He spent years working on the railroad in California; he was away from the reservation. But many people of my grandfather's and even of my father's generation, when the time comes, they're going to retire back home. Well, he does. And he's quite a lady's man and a little bit of a show-off. He gets into some trouble, and he's told he has to leave. And he intends to go to Phoenix, but he accidentally ends up in Tucson. And who he meets up with are Mexican Indians, some of whom are Yaquis from the mountains. But others are remnants of other entire cultures and tribes that were destroyed, early on, after the Europeans came in. And it [the novel] is ambitious because it's saying, "Well, suppose we get rid of the reservation; let's even get you from any of that when you're seven; let's do that." And different groups: "Let's tear you from Yaqui history, and let's form something more indefinite, you now, and let's add this guy who got kicked out. So then, should we say that these people aren't living on the reservation, or never had a reservation, or were there but never really believed?" So what does that mean? And to watch them as characters, and see how they behave; and that's where we pick up. So that's what it's about. So it's really ambitious. It goes back in time.

It's called *Almanac of the Dead*, which is a reference to the Mayan almanacs which are not only used for planting, not just for auspicious planting, but it would also tell you about famine and death, revolution and conquest. They are fragmentary manuscripts, and of course what have I done? I have created a character who has a fragment that nobody else has. So I get to say what it is. So there's only four Mayan codexes. There's the Madrid, the Paris, the Mexico City, and the Dresden copies of Mayan almanacs. And they're just fragments. They're written in Latin or Spanish by Indians, Mayans, full-bloods. They are the first generation of young children, Indian children, young boys, that the priests put in schools. And they could read and write. When they went home, the elders saw that the oral tradition could not be maintained, where you have genocide on this scale. We have no guarantee in this new world of the European conquest, we have no guarantee that the three of us [my two sons and I] will still live.

The old folks thought about it, had people explain to them what writing was. It dawned on them; it's a tool. It's a tool. So in my novel, they call in a person who is trained in the omens. And the old people, men and women, sit down and say, this is how we see it: we've got to start writing. In fact, they theorize something similar to what actually happened, except that my characters have a fragment that no one else has.

Another thing that happens is, I have caretakers of these few pages. At different times they've had to change them around, so they won't be found. Because you do know that the priests would destroy those materials. Some of the keepers have been well-meaning, but they have encoded, they have made a narrative that isn't really the entire narrative. They made a narrative that's a code narrative. And so it makes it extremely strange. What the characters end up with in the contemporary times is a strange bundle, a few fragments of which are originals, but many have traveled and been hidden and stolen and lost. In the novel, there's not that many pages where you actually get to see much of that. But that's in there too.

So I can do anything I want in pre-Columbian times. I'm not even going to call it Mayan. And then because the people believe that these almanacs projected into the future, I can write about a dream I had, which is that the helicopters come from Mexico en route to Tucson, full of American soldiers; that a great battle in this hemisphere will come down. But I connect it to hundreds of years of exploitation of the Native American people here. And I see Marxism as being here, but no better than Christianity. Certainly there are some Marxists, as there are some Catholic nuns and priests, who do some very good things. And I even have a character who actually assassinates—I haven't done it yet—but he's going to assassinate a sort of intellectual Marxist. He's an Indian, and he's very primitive, sort of wonderful, because he just says, "These guys don't want to listen to those guys." Back to the old thing, which is very simpleminded in a way, that it's "our land." And of course, he's a politician; his name is the Ugly One. He says, "We're not interested in any fucking ideology that these outsiders have, we're interested in love." And I don't know about the rest of it, but I'm working hard.

I definitely identify much more with that older generation—so maybe I am a leftover. In terms of the evolution of an ideology, if you want to look at political ideology, I have an awful lot of the old folks' point of view left in me. And I find that in my attraction for the stories, and places, and things I read. There's a lot I don't know. But as a writer and as a person, I like to think of myself in a more old-fashioned sense, the way the old folks felt, which was, first of all you're a human being; secondly you originate from somewhere, and from a family, and a culture. But first of all, human beings. And in order to realize the wonder and power of what we share, we must understand how different we are too, how different things are. I'm really intrigued with finding out similarities in conditions, and yet divergences in responses, of human beings. I'm really interested in that. Without forgetting that first of all, before we can ever appreciate what's the same, we have really to love and respect and be able to internalize freedom of expression.

Gerald Vizenor

Gerald Vizenor was born in 1934 in Minnesota. Of mixed French and Chippewa descent, he is an enrolled member of the Minnesota Chippewa Tribe, White Earth Reservation. Vizenor had a difficult childhood as a consequence both of his family's poverty and his father's murder, which was never solved. These events of his early years, Vizenor calls "metaphors and auto-biographical myths." He incorporates them into his use of the pastiche story, in which grim dramatic events are filtered through Vizenor's subtle, yet incisive, sense of humor.

For three years during the 1950s, Vizenor served in the U.S. Army in Japan. He later studied at New York University and the University of Minnesota, from which he subsequently graduated. Vizenor has been an active organizer in Minnesota Indian communities, serving as director of Inter-Cultural Programs at Park Rapids, Minnesota, and of the American Indian Employments and Guidance Center in Minneapolis. He has taught at Bemidji State University in Bemidji, Minnesota, the University of Minnesota, and the University of California, Berkeley. Currently he teaches literature and American studies at the University of California, Santa Cruz.

A journalist for several years for the Minneapolis Tribune, *Vizenor has written three novels:* Darkness in Saint Louis Bearheart *(1978),* Griever: An American Monkey King in China *(1987), and* The Trickster of Liberty *(1988). He has also published several mixed-genre books about the interrelationships between Indians and whites, such as* Wordarrows: Indians and

Gerald Vizenor

Whites in the New Fur Trade *(1978) and* The People Named the Chippewa: Historical Narratives *(1984)*.

The interview took place on September 10, 1985, in Vizenor's office at the University of California, Berkeley. His words flowed unrelentingly, as if he were not answering my questions but, rather, telling his own narrative, a new "wordmaker," flicking "wordarrows" of humor, sometimes quite a trickster, absolutely a compassionate one.

LC   Will you speak about the storytelling tradition and tribal history in your novels?

VIZENOR   All right. You can't understand the world without telling a story. There isn't any center to the world but a story. I want to distinguish "story." It's not a rehearsed or repeated story, it's a visual reference to experience. In fact I don't know many people, Indian people, who don't tell stories; I mean it's really extraordinary that people don't. Yet there are some people who may be a little shy about it, but if they don't tell, they know how to listen, so they understand. And I think the telling and listening are a little different. It's not a kind of stand-up comedy or vaudeville story, you know, which has a recognizable conflict, punch line, and resolution, but the stories, I believe, are much more humanistic; they grow out of real or imagined experience, both those are real or true, or mythic. I'm talking about contemporary stories now, not the sacred or origin stories that reveal experience in play or how people perceive reality. But those stories come out of a visual reference, and what I mean by visual is not television or films but recollection of multiple senses of an experience so that actually when you call upon an experience in memory and when you decide to tell a story from memory you can tell it from a number of points of view; I mean you see it and hear it and feel it, and you can just step in and talk about it and it takes a different shape or a different bit of humor. I think some of the best stories which have a humanity in them, which have life in them, are centered in a visual memory.

Now, I think some storytellers can develop a visual memory; they can actually bring together from imagination visual events and even mix them up and come up with another story. It's not

something that can be analyzed, at least for a long time. I'm
sure that eventually scientists will be able to focus on the actual
biochemical events, connections, that take place, as well as the
spiritual energy, and they may even be able to map how all these
things take place. It's going to require an incredible computer—
a computer a hundred times, a thousand times, larger than they
can even imagine. And by then they'll probably realize it doesn't
make any difference—that the best computer's your own head
anyway.

LC   What about tribal history in your novels?

VIZENOR   Well, I do work into everything I write so-called historical
events, and I say so-called because some of the historical events
would be obtained from either Indian writers or from Indian
storytellers and other events are from non-Indian historians, so
that they would be either, in the worst example, colonial, and
probably the best example would be methodological histories. I
do work in details where I think it's necessary for recognition of
place and especially where there's conflict; for example, I like
to establish conflict in a story out of a real historical place and
then bring in two people in the contentional conflict with a
real historical background and then just travel with them. I put
myself there; I'll meet them, I'll observe what kind of conflict
they're in. If I'm identifying with one character or the other, I
may become the person imaginatively or I'll be with them as a
witness. And then I'll just move along and it'll work out.

Now, it's not quite that easy because there's also a printed
page, and so then I have to work on the printed page how this
looks, how it feels; it can't be as repetitive as an oral story, or the
reader will get bored with too much repetition. I think there's
quite a debate about that in translation—I'm not translating,
but I mean in translation. There's a great debate about that, and
where it's translation I agree that the repetition should not be ex-
cluded on the printed page. But since I'm writing imaginatively,
I'm writing, telling a story in print, for a reader, and so there are
certain devices in writing and in the printed text that require
a different attention than the oral story. So it's not just a mere
translation of what I'm thinking or what I observe my character
doing; I then have to actually construct a written form. And I

pay attention to many things in that. I don't like repetition of event unless that's my purpose by ritual reference for a mnemonic kind of reference. But I also become very careful not to repeat verbs and nouns and not to draw attention to the language by accident, where a reader will stop and say, "I just saw that word too many times" and so it's a distraction. I'm getting better at that; I mean I notice in my early writing I'm not as skilled as I am now in that attention to the phrases or the structure or syntax.

LC   In *Wordarrows* you say that Indians "are touched into tribal being with words" and that "the arrowmakers and wordmakers survive in the word wars with sacred memories while the factors in the new fur trade separate themselves in wordless and eventless social and political categories."[1] Would you like to comment further on that?

VIZENOR   That's fantastic! Who said that? Give me that citation. Well, obviously I pay a great respect to N. Scott Momaday for that wonderful story of the arrowmaker in *The Way to Rainy Mountain*, and in that story, if you remember, he, Momaday, talks about the arrowmaker who sees through a seam in the tepee a person looking in on him, and the key there is that he says then in his own language, If you understand me, I mean, if you know my word, you're here. If you don't recognize what I'm saying you're about to be shot in the head. An obvious, simple demonstration of the power of language. And that's a powerful idea, but of course we're all speaking English, or most of us, so the rules of speech are much more complicated. People can lie and smile at the same time. They can mean the opposite of what they say. So it's a much more complicated verbal act of survival, and words take on a much more complex and subtle level of power. I mean, we imagine ourselves, we create ourselves, we touch ourselves into being with words, words that are important to us. As children we're touched into being by learning our environment in words.

In a recent story I have a character whose mother taught him the language. His father was opposed to English, forbade him to speak English; he was trying to hold on to two things. One, he was trying to hold on to the security of his way; secondly, he didn't want his children to speak English because he was trying to hold on to his own fears. They'd be different, they'd be more powerful. The mother, however, conspired and she would write words that she found in magazines—since she didn't speak English very well herself—she would print these words on leaves, then she spread them out on the snow and the children would go find them and make a sentence out of the words on leaves. Now the sentences came out unqualified; I mean they were subject and maybe an object; they were very direct statements.

That's how one character I just wrote about learned English. And in many of my stories I work on this idea of how people take in a language, take in the word. Does the word come with the whole thing? I mean, do you take the word in with the object, with leaf, which would be of course a very concrete kind of language? So that if you say that word, you know in concrete sound and in printed word that that visually represents that? That's a very simple and powerful way to learn language. And what I mean by that in contrast to the anthropologists or the colonists is that theirs is an abstract language; it's been borrowed from all over the world. It isn't connected to this land here, to this place; of course neither is it for Indian speakers in English. But do they come to it with their place in it and their tribal words connected to it so there's some transference in cognates to the English words which fit the same experience? But the colonists and travelers speak an abstract language—it's air. It's rich and powerful, it's very romantic, often ideological, extremely abstract; it's difficult to find the verbs in it, because the nouns carry the action. I mean, this isn't true, but to exaggerate, it would be turning pronouns into verbs. They don't do anything but you just verbalize them to show that they're moving, that they're in progress and of course they're not doing anything. I mean, there isn't any concrete verb; there isn't any action that you can feel. I'm again exaggerating.

So, what I mean by being touched into being is that when we imagine ourselves we have to find the words that we like to say about ourselves. I touch myself into being with my own dreams and with my imagination. I am what I say I am, and I emphasize I am as a state of being, and I gather all those words that feed and nurture my imagination about my being. Now, such an act is extremely egoistical, and it may be more characteristic of woodland culture than Pueblo. But cultures are different and I'm writing from mixed-blood, woodland cultural point of view. The songs among the Chippewa, for example, many of them, you know are very egoistical, I mean dream songs: "clouds love to hear me sing." What could be more egoistical than that, but it's a wonderful idea. An old woman at Red Lake sings, "I am as beautiful as the roses," when in fact she's a very ugly person, but she imagined herself as a lovely thought. So we imagine ourselves into being. I mean obviously we have to mature beyond that, but we're touched into being with words. And not just descriptive words, which I think are potentially passive and romantic. Many of our descriptive words in English or nouns are borrowed from about three thousand different languages. Just take the names of our ordinary food at breakfast and we've combined half a dozen cultures. So it's hard to find the place for those words, but if you focus on the being "I am" rather than "I have" [you see that there] has been a shift in our culture.

Erich Fromm points out in *To Have or to Be* that our culture, our American culture, has shifted from states of being to states of ownership. I suppose it naturally follows in a consumer culture that very soon, with so much available, you consume the words too—you'd own everything. We now say, "I have a child, I have a family, I have a wife," rather than "I am, I am, I am" or "We are." So the idea of being is important, and verbs are important to being.

We wear masks with names. You can't wear a mask with action. For example, it's exciting to observe the masks that people wear, especially in Berkeley; I'm enchanted, thrilled, by the masks that people wear here. Now, some of them actually wear concrete masks; they actually put something on, not just makeup and cosmetics, but they actually put something on: hair, glasses, wigs, real masks of different faces, clothing, limp, songs. Everything they know becomes a kind of mask or metaphor for who they want to be or don't want to be. And it's interesting and fascinating and maybe the mask is enough for many people—maybe enough to relate to the mask. People either want to hide or to be somebody else and that may be enough to just meet on the mask. But it's not enough to find out if there's any being there, if there's any substance in the person, if there's any compassion, and ultimately that must make people very insecure—surrounded by masks and not knowing what the masks will do if they have to act. So I'm more interested in the verbs, in the acts of people, because therein is the truth of them, their being. Their masks are fascinating and maybe the mask corresponds directly to the action, but we don't know that until we see the act, and some people are better actors too.

LC We have just seen *Harold of Orange*, your film based on your script. The trickster, the transformer, the clown—the cultural hero is the most important character in your fiction and also in your filmscript. You define him as "a compassionate and imaginative character," so different from the trickster of the anthropologists. Would you comment on that?

VIZENOR Everything in anthropology is an invention and an extension of the cultural colonialism of Western expansion. I don't see anthropology as doing a disservice to anyone, but the way I see anthropology is much different from the way anthropologists see themselves. And the way they see Indians is much different from the way I see them. Now, you would expect that setup would have some mutual respect because reasonable people, as the lawyers say, can disagree, but not so. Anthropologists believe they are right and what they have methodologically constructed is true because of the socioscientific method. I, on the other hand, think that their methodology is narrow, bigoted, and colonial, however objective they pretend to be, and that most of what they say, if not all of what they have said about tribal people, is at best, at very best, bullshit. Now, at best being bullshit, there still is some room for humor. See? But they don't even have any humor. I mean, they don't have anything. They got a bundle of bad methodologies, methodologies which have distorted the human spirit since anthropologists have been eagerly pursuing the invention of culture—and they invented culture. Culture doesn't exist; they invented it. They need culture so they can get Ph.D.s and gain power in universities. And people who have that kind of power control culture, because they control the definitions, the symbols, and the masks they've constructed about culture.

I'm going to borrow an idea from Susan Sontag that I think

is just wonderful—if their invention is like a photograph or a snapshot, Sontag says that what's happened in the snapshot or in the photograph is that there's a power in it because you capture an image, and if that image begins to represent something, then, because it has power, you can really change the images and people might believe that you've actually changed social conditions. And, of course, you haven't done anything. You've just changed the photos; you just shuffle the images and symbols.

So I see anthropologists as not even that sophisticated. I mean; they don't even have any interesting symbols; they borrowed everything, or stole it. They haven't even taken any photographs that are worth a damn; they don't even have a good collection of art of their own. They've borrowed everything from tribal culture and then they've imposed identification tags or methodological inventions of cultures and maintained those inventions so as to maintain their own power. Now, there could be some humor in that, but most anthropologists deny the possibility of humor and play. They are tragic people who have a tragic worldview and they just can't allow play. If they allow play, they might have to face the fact that they're losing their power over their images and control of cultures. So as a result they contribute to this idea that Indians are this kind of a person, and then people like Vizenor and other mixed-bloods aren't Indian. That follows because if I'm peering through the seams and punching holes in the shroud and changing the patches on their methodology, or challenging at least—that sounds pretty arrogant. I'm sure it won't have much effect at all—but whatever my criticism the defense against that would be that I'm not Indian and what do I know. I don't know any more than an anthropologist and that's true—I don't know, but I don't pretend to invent the culture, either. I do my best to imagine myself, and my acts of imagination, I believe, leave open the possibility for human and spiritual experience.

LC   What about the trickster as a compassionate and imaginative character?

VIZENOR   I emphasize compassionate because Paul Radin and others have identified the trickster as being asocial and amoral at best. And they've interpreted a lot of his acts as being disruptive, and yes, they are, but no one has emphasized that these acts are compassionate. I see them as compassionate. I mean, the trickster doesn't kill people. If he symbolically wrecks people's lives—that's symbolic. A trickster in practice, in an imaginative practice, is not killing people, but we're led to believe that the trickster is equivalent to a used-car salesman and if you don't watch out—you know it's "buyer beware" for the con-man in American culture—you'll be tricked out of your money. Well, that's not a tribal trickster idea; that's a consumption thing and that's tricks for evil purposes and domination. A trickster doesn't seize power; he doesn't control power in tribal cultures; it's a compassionate act; he disrupts, makes people very uncomfortable, unhappy, may even threaten them, but he never maintains an army, he never has established a university; he holds credentials which others must study in order to maintain their power in the field or academe.

In other words, the trickster doesn't want to be an anthropologist. And the problem is that anthropologists have wanted trickster to become anthropologists. They want everybody to be an anthropologist so it increases their power. I like kicking around anthropologists—it's really fun. Anthropology is a material creation; a trickster is a spiritual, imaginative act. Anthropologists have things; tricksters are.

LC   In the traditional Anishinabe creation myth, the earthdiver brings up five grains of sand from the water to form the earth, a central metaphor in your work for the contemporary earthdivers, the mixed-bloods, who are both animals and tricksters, both white and tribal. A new urban Turtle Island?

VIZENOR   Yeah, it's a play on the metaphor of the earth being, after the flood, made on the back of a turtle so it won't sink again, and the trickster creation story is a secular version of creation. There are many versions. It's not the sacred one; the sacred ones of course are the families of creation, I mean, the great families—and their winds and animals and birds are all part, are somehow related to the creation of humans. But the trickster's is a greater challenge; he's trying to keep his nose above the flood; and, as any trickster would say, "it ain't easy." So he's a survivor in the sense of comedy and comic worldview. He's not trying to establish a nation or a state or an automobile agency or an anthropology department. What the trickster wants to do in creating the new world is just get along; and he's not a tragic hero, he's a comic survivor. But he barely makes it. I mean, here the animals who he thought could do the job for him didn't, and there was this scrawny little muskrat who he didn't hold a lot of faith in, in the first place, which to me suggests wonderful contradictions of chance, and they all come back to life and nobody ever lives happily ever after. That's a romantic's projection.

So my argument is this, it's pretty obvious in my work, and as we've talked too, that stories are not static; there are no scriptural versions of oral traditional stories. There are great variations. A storyteller was an artist, an imaginative person. He brought himself into being and listeners into being with his imagination. Surely some people were better than others, better in the sense that it worked out better with listeners. Some people find different listeners and they're better with this group than with that group. I mean, there's a lot of variation, a lot of room. But here comes an anthropologist, records one version; an anthropologist-linguist translates it, and these translations unfortunately become objects, material objects. And then they become kind of scripture, as if it's a litany, that you have to subscribe to and repeat and memorize. And that's not my idea. That's an idea of death—that's not an idea of imagination and life.

If a culture lives, it changes, it always changes. If a people live, they imagine themselves always and in a new sense. And here we are in the city, and people are still trying to figure out what was the past. Well, there isn't any past, we're it, and I am, and I'm on the intersection; and I'm finding my way through traffic and I'm going to tell some stories about it. Just as people who found their way through the imaginative traffic a thousand years ago figured out their stories as comic acts of survival.

I'd like to do two things in storytelling: one, I'd like to discover myself in the story as imaginative; I'd like to feel good about it, at least about the trickster ideas in stories. I'd like to imagine myself moving through certain contradictions and conflicts with good humor and maybe a lesson here and there and slipping past it without being damaged by it.

LC   As a mixed-blood as well?

VIZENOR   Oh, good point, because mixed-bloods, in a sense, I think, are driven to the recognition of change with a difference. There aren't any choices unless they lie to themselves. I suppose there are a number of people who pretend or lie. If you are darkskinned it's easier to lie. So I think, if you are lightskinned and you're mixed-blood, then it's obvious and you can't deal with it. That's only true in a racist society. In a society that doesn't establish meaning on the basis of skin color, then it wouldn't make any difference. But we live in a society where one of the first categories to divide people, after sex, is skin color. And so that's the most significant category in American culture and in many parts of the world. So the mixed-blood is driven to the possibilities of being trickster, though not all are. And then trickster-earthdiver, because wherever we go we're trying to put together a new act of survival, a new imaginative state of being, a new way to deal with things. Now, I can't be too pragmatic about this. The whole idea falls apart if you say to me or if you ask me, "But with such a view, how can you actually graduate from college? And how can you be a banker?" And I don't know these things. Those are pragmatic things that people work out for themselves, by the moment. But I think the idea of a trickster and the life energy of a compassionate trickster-earthdiver is a constant stimulation to imagine oneself, and I think it works everywhere. It works for me on the page and sometimes in real life. Remember, I mean on the page is not real life, but I think it works both places. I think it's a healthy worldview because it's comic, it leaves much more room for human imagination and for spiritual connections, and I think it's just better for the heart —the physical heart. I think it lasts longer. That and pasta and olive oil!

LC   In your books you focus your attention on the urban reservation more than ever coping with a dominant society. Does it lead more than ever to "cultural suicides," as you say in your poem "Indians at the Guthrie," or does it create "a new consciousness of coexistence"? [2]

VIZENOR   Very perceptive selection of quotes revealing the ultimate contradictions in my work. That's very good. Let's see. Yeah, you've selected the two contradictions or representative ideas of contradictions.

LC   Perhaps you wrote these sentences in different periods.

VIZENOR   Yes and no. They are both idealistic or romantic statements: one's tragic-romantic and the other's a comic idealism statement, idealism that we can dedicate ourselves to, and then become significant and important people. And so they're both very idealistic—one being very tragic, of course. Yes, the cultural suicides go on in the city every day. People have been so beaten that they have no energy left to know how to imagine themselves. And they only know how to be victims—not just mixed-bloods or Indians but loads of other people. We see the victims all over, and it's disheartening and sad because you can't just stop someone in the street who's been a victim for ten, twenty years and try to cheer them up—there's no place to cheer them, there's no trick or intersection left for them to laugh easily or even perceive their own tragedy or comedy. It's very sad and it's extremely tragic so I'm moved by that obviously. Quite a bit of my writing is revealed therein—people don't like to read that.

Mostly younger Indians who are eager to present a more successful and "healed" image are quite critical of me focusing too often on the tragic and the downtrodden and the victims. Now, I don't that much, but I have, especially when I was a journalist, and I think it's because at that point in my life, I was discovering, for myself as a journalist, even some things I didn't want to know. And even within my own family I had some sense of experience; my father was murdered, and so in the discovery of that by questioning people about that time—it happened when I was quite young—and later when I investigated, there's a darkness in me. There's a darkness in me and there's light in me. I think I have a blazing light, at times. I think I have a blazing wit, at times. And sometimes it shows in spontaneous stories and sometimes it shows on the printed page. In both cases I need someone to hear me or read me and to appreciate it. And the darkness I don't think people want to hear that much. Some people will read it; fewer people will hear it. So I don't talk much about the darkness, but I do still write about it at times.

Probably the darkest visions are in *Darkness in Saint Louis Bearheart*. So the darkness is in me, too. And as I said today, we all have it, we all have the darkness and light, or we have good and evil. And I think on the outside if you view writing or imagination as cathartic—I don't—but if you view it that way, you could observe that Vizenor balances his intensities of darkness and light on the printed page. I think that's kind of corny, but I could see someone actually saying that. And then I'd say, "Huh, imagine that."

I think another thing is that I've been able to escape the experiences I've had as a community organizer. I internalized a lot of pain and suffering—I don't want to make myself a big person out of this now—you can't help it. And there's so much need and it's so immediate. This second, right there, that very minute that I could laugh about, someone sees as the major obstacle of their life. That second, right there, hardly even counts, but for me a second like that might be a great source of humor; for another person it becomes an absolutely life-threatening instant. And I've had people just walk into an office I opened on Franklin Avenue with nothing left in their psychic energy but that last effort to open the door. And often all you can say, really, is, "Too bad." You can't solve people's lives; you can only work with humor and material. You can only provide food and material things; you can't do much with the spirit. Other people can; I think other people pretend to do things with the spirit. Obviously, psychoanalysis hasn't been very successful for anybody—even people who live in Austria. But I'm getting off the point.

So I've taken in a lot of experience, some of it in my own family but a lot of it in the street. And to a certain extent I do regret focusing on it too much. I've been so angry that it's unbelievable sometimes. I've been so angry sometimes that I'm afraid of myself. I remember—I'll give you an example: a woman called me in the morning—I wrote about this—and said, "I just stopped drinking. My children have been taken away by the state. I've been thrown out of my apartment. It's winter. I have no money, no winter coat, no food. I'm in a phone booth; I just spent my last dime to call you." Well, that's got to be a joke, come on, who—at eight o'clock in the morning—has got all those things going? You know, that's a bit much. Well, I thought, at that second I guess, lucky for her I was there. I might have stopped off and visited some friends and I wouldn't have been there and that second would have passed. She would have done something else. She'd have gotten along, but she'd have done something else. So I was there and I went down and met her, and she needed medical care so I took her down to the hospital, and they wouldn't treat her; they wouldn't deal with her, and the man said, "We don't deal with people who don't have an address." She'd just been thrown out her apartment. I said, "Well, I'll give her an address." Then he wouldn't deal with her because her husband's was her address. Another problem. Patriarchal interpretations—your residence is where your husband is unless you declared legally otherwise. And I was so angry with that and with similar things like that, and that particular day I was close to pounding that person, so close, it took everything I had to hold back. And I didn't dare say another word because one word would have opened it and I'd have just gone—right through the word. So what I had to do to balance myself was, I had to—I used to swim a lot, I occasionally do now, but I used to swim much more then—rush to the swimming pool and I swam for an hour. I told her to wait in the waiting room. I said, "I'm past being able to do anything. Don't go away. Another hour isn't going to make any difference. Just stay there." And I ran off and I swam and it was a form of meditation, and then I came back and I was in very good form, and I took her home and then I wrote that story. I wanted to show that there aren't any miracles to this. You pick the moment, the second, and you want the world to change with you, and it isn't going to do it. In fact it's going to say to you, "Too bad. Stay a victim." And so you just have to re-imagine yourself. And, well, as the story finished, she out of a few choices, chose to be left off at the same phone booth where we'd met, after dinner. I'd see the lightness part humor—as an act of survival, humor as balance, and play as imagination and avoidance of boredom and all that. And most of the day probably is just spent doing ordinary things like reading the newspaper and sorting my mail.

LC And what about coexistence?

VIZENOR Equal coexistence? Yeah. I think it's a flashy phrase. It's idealistic.

LC The title of your book *The People Named the Chippewa* sounds very ironical, since Chippewa is the name given to the Anishinabeg by the colonists. You also make a distinction between history and identity, between tribal perspectives and, again, those of anthropologists. As in some other instances concerning the anthropologists' work, do they fail in interpreting the American Indian world and thought?

VIZENOR The anthropologists?

LC Right.

VIZENOR Dead failures. They've never been right once.

LC Just speaking of your book.

VIZENOR I go after them there. I've been playful before; I was very serious and quite aggressive in that book. In two ways. One, my opinion. And then secondly I actually pulled apart two books to demonstrate how absolutely absurd their historical and anthropological summaries are about tribal cultures. But there's no stopping them, so we have to figure out how to laugh more. There is no stopping. I suppose they're going to inherit this earth, after all. I think, though, that come the time when we reallocate the properties of the universe I think what I want to leave to the anthropologists, if I have any say then, come the reallotment of this nation, I want to leave for the anthropologists the buildings they're in.

Actually your questions are really good. There's nothing boring in your questions, I can assure you.

LC There's nothing boring in your answers!

VIZENOR Now, that's a good story! What's obvious in this is that I'm establishing in play a kind of binary; it's anthropologists and then play, humor and imagination. I can say dumb things like, "Some anthropologists are my best friends" and stuff like that, and some things I read by anthropologists are really interesting. I think a tremendous disservice has occurred, but I'm not naive about it. Knowledge is power, and there is, as Michel Foucault would say, an archaeology of this knowledge and energy. My point is that it doesn't have anything to do with Indians, and I'd like to just refocus it to where it is. It's a system of power; anthropologists have invented cultures; it doesn't have anything to do with Indians and it's all their business. I think it's interesting as their business. It's very interesting. And they can peek at each other, you know, on either side of the bookshelves. They can hold up their microfiches and change the world through the printed image. And I think they're interesting in their collection of data and the way they sort it and scramble it and reinvent it, but it doesn't have anything to do with tribal people. It never will. And I don't believe it has anything to do with intellectual humanism. That may hurt some people who think that in the study of man, in anthropology, that they're coming closer to a kind of reality of human behavior. I think it separates people. The methodologies of the social sciences separate people from the human spirit. They separate people through word icons, methods that become icons because they're powerful, because they're rewarded by institutions—separate them from a kind of intellectual humanism, an integrity of humanism and the human spirit. And the spontaneity of being alive and being unpredictable and playing. There's nothing more deadly than to have somebody show up with a notebook in the middle of your game.

LC   Speaking about politics and Indians, in *Wordarrows* tribal people refuse to write about their experiences for communist newspapers because "there was too little humor in communist speech."[3] In your words, the members of the American Indian Movement "seem to mimic the romantic pictorial images in old photographs taken by Edward Curtis for a white audience, decorating themselves in pastiche pan-tribal vestments."[4] How do tribal people look at them?

VIZENOR   Well, the obvious thing is that I can't speak for tribal people, but speaking for myself, I've seen some of the radical leaders and others—not just radical; I'm just writing in that case about radicals—who present themselves according to the photographic images that are familiar. It's a costume and a mask, and going back to Susan Sontag again, here we have a power in an image, real social power, political power in an image, and Sontag points out that by taking photographs we're actually capturing the image of people and you can control them with their own images or with these images you possess. There's nothing innocent about the possession of these images. You can determine how people will be seen and how they will be presented with these images. And especially when the images have been constructed, invented too, but constructed.

For example, many of the photographers wanted to photograph Indians to appear to be traditional. They wanted the perfect Indian, before he vanished. They dressed Indians from a trunk, pastiche junk, and in fact there are photographs of Indians who are wearing feather headdresses—feather dusters, because that's all the photographer could find at hand to decorate them with. And Edward Curtis, who is the best-known and the most powerful pictorialist photographer, truly a great photographer and an artist, but not an ethnographer—his are not documentary or ethnographic photographs. He's not photographing Indian people as they are. If he were, he would have had some people driving early automobiles, dressed in ordinary clothes, looking mostly like other people in the areas they live in, but not so. Almost all of Edward Curtis's people look traditional, and wherever something appeared that showed evidence of Western contact, he removed it; in some cases he altered negatives in order to show Indians as being more traditional. Well, my point is that these are powerful images. These images have taught people who Indians are, and you can change these images, in the Sontag tradition, because they are powerful, and it gives the illusion that you're actually changing social conditions. Now, if you're a tribal person and you want to confront or get a piece of all of that or step into the shadow of that photographic image of power, you dress up like the photograph. You'll be instantly recognized.

Probably the greatest expectations for Indians in terms of pan-tribal pastiche is in Europe. Appear in Germany dressed in a business suit as an Indian—forget it. Most parts of the United States too. But dress up in western headdress or western symbols or western costumes or cultural objects and there's instant recognition. And so we noticed that when a lot of Indian people traveled to Europe, they had to travel with outfits. They packed their stuff like any other tourist. People don't dress like that in real life. That's really corny. There aren't any equivalents for it directly, except maybe in child's play where a little girl is wearing high heels or something like that, I don't know. But it's really humorous and playful and of course it goes on, you still see it. Less, though.

LC You mentioned before skin colors; introducing the color wheel in *Earthdivers*, a kind of register of skintones, you satirize America's attitude toward skin color, including also the full-blood and the mixed-blood. Again, "terminal creeds are terminal diseases."[5]

VIZENOR That's the ultimate tragic worldview—a terminal single-minded fascistic formula for the world is terminal. We've seen it everywhere in history, everywhere in Europe, everywhere in America, see bits and parts of it now, still around in some political parties, in some religious movements. And to try to come up with a single idealistic definition of tradition in a tribal culture is terminal. Cultures are not static, human behavior is not static. We are not what anthropologists say we are and we must not live up to a definition. That definition can only be manipulated by fascistic interests. We're very complex human beings, all of us, everywhere, but especially in America and especially among tribal groups and especially mixed-bloods. Mixed-bloods represent the actual physical union of the binary of tribal and Western. In my case it would be that premiere union between the French and the Anishinabeg or Chippewa. And I didn't have any choice in that, but I'm not a victim. I imagine myself in good humor and wish to live a responsible life, and so I'm not going to fall off the edge as some imperfect person just because I'm an accident in history. I could argue the other way and say the accidents in history may be the most imaginative—but that's a racist statement.

LC Will you talk about colonized tribal cultures and the Curtis photographs which you discuss in your essay "Socioacupuncture"?[6]

VIZENOR What I did was borrow an idea from Roland Barthes about the striptease—that it's a titillation down to the point when you take off the last bit of clothing and then it's boring. So there's something in the striptease, not necessarily in the end. So I thought, now that's interesting, because for Indians as they've been colonized by anthropologists and historians and politicians, as they've been colonized, they've lived the opposite of a striptease—they've been dressed up. And it's the dressing up of them that's titillating. The end product is boring, just as it is by taking your clothes off. It's the titillation to the end, and with the Indians, the invention of the Indians, it's the titillation into image.

So I argued that and I used two characters. One is an invented or an imagined persona—could just as well be me—and this imagined persona is talking about Ishi, the California Indian, and then I dissolve time and I bring everybody together at once on the page: Roland Barthes, persona, Ishi, the anthropologist Alfred E. Kroeber, several others anthropologists, Thomas T. Waterman, a linguist, other people who knew Ishi and worked with him here at the university. And then also some of the members of the university regents at the time and then the university president, Benjamin Ide Wheeler, for whom the hall is named. Anyway, brought all these people together at a graduation ceremony at the University of California, and I used real quotations from letters and books written by Alfred Kroeber and others and Saxton Pope, who was Ishi's medical doctor and also a person who wrote about bows and arrows—he was just fascinated with both. I brought all these people together and I used some of their quotes, coming out of their mouth at a graduation ceremony where Ishi was being awarded an honorary PH.D. degree. Now, I wanted to do this because Alfred Kroeber said of Ishi that he was one of the wisest, most profound men he ever knew and that this was intuitive—he just knew these things. So I thought, now, this is really interesting because here is one of the most distinguished minds in American anthropology saying in print that Ishi, an untutored, uneducated, although now institutionalized, Indian, is smarter than he is. Well, now, who should have the PH.D.? You see what I mean? So we give him a PH.D. and everybody's very happy and then we undress, the Indians undress, they take off—they striptease. They do the reverse striptease; they take it all off. They take off the vestments, they take off all the stuff that's in the photographs. They take off all the pastiche and pan-tribal junk and they become real wise people. They get out of the photographs, slowly, so as to titillate the observers.

LC   In the epigraph to "Spacious Treeline in Words" in *Earthdivers* you quote Jacques Derrida's statement "Between the too warm flesh of the literary event and the cold skin of the concept runs meaning" [*Writing and Difference*]. Could you talk of the word cinemas from this point of view?

VIZENOR   You're a very tough reader. That's very good. Well, the mixed-bloods are between [worlds], so's the trickster; he's neither tradition nor antitradition; he's not power or weakness. And a mixed-blood must waver in the blood and it's difficult to waver the page. You have to find some meaning not in the sides but in the seam in between and that's obviously where a mixed-blood, an earthdiver, a trickster, must try and find all meaning, imaginative meaning. It's where the contention is, it's where the energy lies, it's where the focus is, it's where the photographs fall on either side. Perhaps it's a blessing in a way that there aren't any fixed images of the in-between, so, as the deconstructionists might argue, the meaning is in the play; it's in the trace, it's in the difference, it's in what isn't there, and it isn't in the lexical meaning of the word and it's not in the nonlexical meaning of the word. It's in between, it's sort of in between the two words and then it's even in between the definitions of the word, of one word. So a mixed-blood's neither this nor that and neither up nor down, neither wise nor stupid, but it demands an imaginative presentation, since we're not fixed in photographs and we're not fixed in lexicons, and anthropologists have had a hell of a time tacking us to a paper. We're trouble, and I'd rather be trouble than an image.

LC   Speaking about postmodern novels, are there any writers you especially admire or feel affinities with? You know that you are labeled as a postmodern novelist. Are you happy about that?

VIZENOR   I don't know what it means. I think it's easier to understand modern, postmodern, in art and I think to a certain extent that literature, literary critics, have borrowed some ideas from the criticism of art, because the more obvious shift in tradition is in painting or in sculpture than in writing. We're still using the English language, if we're writing in English, and it has a certain grammatical structure so a certain element of tradition. Now, some people have attempted writing which is not familiar syntactical, grammatical construction, but that hasn't gotten very far and that surely isn't identified as postmodern. It's content, characterization, narrative structure which suits the interests of critics who identify things as postmodern.

But I'm not completely sure what it means. Well, first of all let me point out that I lean a bit more toward the margin, toward the deconstruction approach to discovering the play in a word, so just saying that, you see, there's symbolic possibilities in all words. So that's what I mean by that, okay? I also mean by that that I choose words intentionally because they have established multiple symbolic meanings, and sometimes I put them in place so that they're in contradiction, so that you can read it several ways. You can read it just for its surface trace and definition—lexical definition—or you can change the definition in this one and leave that one the same and there's contention or agreement.

I'm not quite that masterful at every level, but there are many places where I deliberately did that and also where I work on the most obvious binaries. Simple, structural stuff—night and day, men and women, dogs and humans, savage and civilized—the simplest binary constructions, but I shift them to multiple meanings. And it depends upon how you want to read it. For example, there are people who are very offended by a scene of a woman having sex with dogs. All right. I answer it in two ways: first of all, you misread it, if you're offended. So it's the way you read it—that's your problem. Reread it, you might find the following things: one, I've told you stories before, other characters have told you stories in the novel about creation possibilities that all life has some relationship—it's a worldview. There have been marriages between animals and humans. And you can accept that on a kind of folk level, mythic level, but here it is, now what do you do? Is it too real? Has it lost its mythic power or is myth just make-believe? Is myth just for fairy-tale movies or is myth a powerful reality, a truth that can be experienced? I believe it can be experienced and I did it on the page. My second statement, to somebody who finds fault with that, is you'd better reread it and then tell me what's wrong with a human being loving an animal. What's wrong with that is Judeo-Christian, not tribal. That doesn't mean that tribal people are sleeping with animals, I don't mean that, but in the story there isn't anything wrong with it. I thought it was a very sensous act of love. I was turned on by it myself. I thought it was cosmically erotic; it was mythically connected, sexually and culturally, and I just think it's a wonderful scene. And on a constellation blanket, no less!

LC   In almost every university there is an American Indian Studies Center. Do you still label them as "the Department of Undecided Studies"?[7]

VIZENOR   Well, that title came out of the realization at the University of Minnesota that in fact most of the Indians attending university there didn't decide what they were going to major in until the last year. So we were joking around one day, a number of us, and we came up with this: we ought to name this the Department of Undecided Studies because nobody can figure it out until they're right up to the last minute, and when they sort of put together what they've got, to see what they can get a degree out of. I think that's changed a bit; I mean, there are still some people who will hang on undeclared as long as they can. But I think it's changed, I think Indians are choosing specific fields and are pursuing many more professional programs, and so they might imagine they're in undecided studies but their practical work is very well decided.

LC   You teach American Indian literature at Berkeley. What's the response you get from your students?

VIZENOR   I'd kind of emphasize the positive aspect. The positive response is that Indian literature is more accessible and more, much more, interesting, and I think there are two reasons. One, the content is more unique and they [the students] like the idea of some guidance in interpreting the narrative. But also I think their statement that Indian literature is more interesting is that we haven't pulled it apart as many English teachers do with literature. I mean, you know it's a kind of specimen rather than living, imaginative work. And I think that's part of the difference, because many people come who have taken courses in the American novel or other cultures and it's pulled apart so mechanically that they don't like reading it; and I don't know anybody in Indian literature who does that, at least not teaching it every quarter. Maybe it'll come to that, I don't know. The other thing I think is that in American Indian studies here—

again the positive parts; there are some negative things too—
many students appreciate taking our courses because they say
the faculty are accessible. And I never thought too much about
that; I thought at first it was kind of a con. You know, there's one
of those pleasant students' flattering cons, and it feels good and,
okay, tell me more. But I think there's some truth in it. As I've
been around the university, you can hardly find anybody in and
the students are always complaining about not being able to find
faculty members. And I think they're off doing their own business and I think for various reasons teachers in Indian studies
have given more time to it, probably out of their own insecuri-
ties, out of their interests, out of their anxieties of maintaining
the program and the job and maybe even the love of it, and so as a
result they're more accessible and students do appreciate it, they
really do. And they comment on it. Not only personally, but they
often say so in the course evaluation at the end of the term. So
I think that's the positive part of Indian literature classes—that
it's more accessible, there are less obstacles in theory. That may
only be because there aren't that many theories about Indian
literature yet. You see what I mean? I'm not trying to romanti-
cize it, but the time may come when we're about as dense and
obstacle-ridden as any other literature, but right now we're not.
The literature's good and it's new, it's a new literature for many
people, they've never even considered anything like it. And it's
a bit of a key. In just one course you can read half a dozen books
and have a real key to a culture and a literature, and it's new and
different so there's some excitement in that.

LC   What do you think of non-Indian readers and critics of your work
and of American Indian literature in general?

VIZENOR   For the most part I've been greatly impressed by non-Indian
teachers, writers, and critics because they're very dedicated.
Well, there are a few people, I'm sure, here and there who have
made a name for themselves on this or that, but they don't
last long and it's never been a serious thing and you couldn't
in any way characterize what's going on in non-Indian writing
about Indian literature in that way. Those postcolonial roman-
tics don't last long, you know; word gets around and it ends
pretty fast. There's a tremendous dedication, and for the most

part I can't say that any of the people who have given their energy and scholarship to Indian literature have gotten much money out of it. You don't get promoted by paying attention to Indian literature, so for the most part you really have to have your promotions established before you do this because it might even work against you. I might be overstating that, but I think it's pretty well established that you don't win a whole lot of points on your committees with fooling around in Indian literature, as interesting as it might be.

So on the one hand I have just had a kind of flattering complimentary response and I'm so pleased that so many people and more and more take it seriously, and it's a very serious scholarship, which is impressive—doesn't mean I agree with it, but it's impressive. It's the kind of stuff you can argue with, honestly, respectfully, and not come up feeling raped or victimized. It is really serious and it's good stuff, and it's open play, in the best sense.

LC   Can you see in your work an evolution concerning themes, style, and so on?

VIZENOR   Well, in writing and publishing I first started in poetry and short story and then did a lot of poetry and then essays, journalism, a lot of journalism, then back to a combined kind of fiction—as people say, narrative fiction with real events, narratives with historical events—and then these peculiar things like *Earthdivers*, stuff like that, experimental writing. But I've shifted to a more direct narrative style in the latest novel, *Griever*, and I'm practicing shifts in identity through action and pronouns rather than through shifts in time, other prose where you just make a radical shift from mythic to temporal, great shift in time, which I think is tough for readers. But now I'm not doing much of that. Now I'm trying to carry a straight narrative with a story, a little bit of suspense in some simple ways, so there is what appears to be conclusion. Nothing is closure, but certain ambitions to know certain things will be satisfied. That's not an end of anything but it's a comic circle. And rather than shifting time, what I'm working on now is that there are shifts in time, but I'm not just doing it by breaks from mythic to calendar time. I'm actually doing it in narrative voices; I mean, the reader's coming with me in historical present or immediate past, and we just walk right into it so the reader sees it coming, and you just walk right into it with the character who's now "wavering," and then you come out the other end. Might be a problem there in this new novel, where a reader may forget in the middle that he just walked in there. None of these parts are more than a page, but sometimes a reader gets in the middle and forgets that I just showed him the tunnel and now we're coming out the other side.

I've also been working on pronoun shifts and I'm fascinated by that. In *Bearheart*, for example, I was more dramatic about the sex differences, and it actually had transsexual surgery, wearing masks and visually changing identity, very obviously and dramatically just reversing—symbolic reversals, which is more of the theater gesture. I can't say that I planned any reversals like that, but I noticed in this book I've had either two or three sex reversals, but they're not in mask or drama. It's not so theatrical; it's just pronouns. The same action is carried out, but I just shift the pronoun. I just twist the pronoun and so you don't even have to see it; you don't have to read it. One is the sex scene—it isn't realized, but a character's been very stimulated for a certain period of time and now he's pursuing this person, and then it turns to fantasy. The person has disappeared and so he's just thinking about what he'd do if he could and then right in the middle of what he's thinking about, the pronoun shifts and it's "she, she." And I think what I'm doing is the same thing I did with dog and woman. It doesn't make any difference, you know what I mean, it's just pronouns. That's about all it is. We've invested so much in pronouns.

LC   Would you describe your writing process?

VIZENOR   I prefer to write in the morning, and for the obvious, almost cliché reason, I don't like to talk with people or to be distracted by anything else, since it does shift a whole group of references to some other event or place, so it's hard to get back. It's all right if I've been working two or three hours; then I can go do things because I just keep my mind on that, and I just pretend to carry out these other things and then come back. But I can't start with something else; it's much more difficult to come back. So I work in the morning for the most part. In the evening quite often I'll reread and make changes. In the past I would type directly on a manual typewriter, so it was a pretty ragged page, and then I would rewrite all over it and then retype it. Then I shifted occasionally to actually longhand and then that would be a little more comprehensible. And then I'd make all kinds of changes just while I'm typing and reading my own handwriting. And one reason I started back to this again for a time was because it was just too fatiguing typing that much, and I couldn't type fast enough—I was just hamming up the keys and it's too distracting, and an electric typewriter wasn't any better—it's too noisy. So I'm writing by hand now, but I'm writing so fast that if I don't transcribe it within a couple of hours, I can't recognize it. You know, it's that rapid—just totally unreadable. But now I've gone to a word processor. This recent novel was the first thing I've written on it and I get it started by writing free hand —I get the idea started—and then I move to the word processor. But sometimes I just keep going in writing, I just can't get out of handwriting. Then I'll transcribe it to a word processor.

LC   Could you talk a little bit more about your new novel *Griever* and about other works in progress?

VIZENOR   I can't think of anything I've written that I didn't intend to write, and *Griever*'s the first book I've done that I didn't intend to write. Everything else I've intended to write. My wife, Laura Hall, and I were going to China to teach and I was not going to work on anything, just read and teach and take in this unusual experience. I had no interest in or no idea of writing; I saw it as too superficial. I'm not going to China to write a book, that's crazy. Every other dingbat's going over there to tell the world about their experience. That's so kitsch, embarrassing. But, we were there about a month and we were taken to a Chinese opera, and by chance it was [about] the Monkey King, and in the middle of it I was just overwhelmed by the Monkey King trickster. They [the Chinese and American Indian tricksters] were first cousins and they've spent a lot of time with each other in the world. And I was just—I felt so excited by this—that this Monkey King has survived the most incredible radical changes a nation could have ever imagined to go through, and now here he is being performed in a communist-socialist state, highly bureaucratized, and here he is, and he is still loved, this wonderful wacky Monkey King. And the Monkey King was doing exactly the things that the woodland trickster was doing—upsetting, distracting, refocusing people who have power, challenging power, seeking ways to be immortal because he was bored being a mortal—just wonderful things.

So it was very fortunate for me that there was a Chinese-American teacher there, my good fortune, because he was born in Tianjin, where we were teaching, and left when he was an adolescent and was educated in the United States. He is a professor and he was back teaching briefly and consulting, and he was raised on the Monkey King—I mean, that was classical literature, and he told me all about it, bought me a book, and that sort of thing. So it was my good fortune that he was there to answer questions, because no one else could.

So that started the book, and what I did was brought an American like myself—I mean I wasn't going to write about China but I was going to write about a trickster who gets it on in China. And I didn't have to go one step past my own experience. I didn't have to write about the Chinese. I just wrote about me as a trickster. So the events are real from my experience, some embellished—both ways: some embellished more and some embellished less. I mean you embellish it by also eliminating some of the obvious contradictions to make it more plausible. And then some imagined scenes which just pleased me because "What could be crazier than what we're doing?" we'd say, and then we'd decide what could be crazier, and they were wonderful stories but in the end we'd say, "No, what we're doing is a hell of a lot crazier than what we can imagine." It really was unusually crazy. So that's the novel and it has a little adventure in it, where there's a killing, actually, a death—not so much Who did it? but Why? And then [there is] an earlier story that's unraveled in this contemporary contention of the trickster in China trying to get along in a bureaucracy.

The Chinese, at first, find the trickster embarrassing—the Americans hate him—he's total embarrassment. You can imagine how the State Department would appreciate him. They would love to export him or execute him. And the Chinese are embarrassed at first too, but they deal with embarrassment in a different way; they are very friendly, but out of their mouths they say, "Wacko bourgeois." But then they loved the trickster. Once they recognized him in the category of the Monkey King, they loved him. He could do anything, and he was compassionate about it. I mean, they knew he wasn't going to destroy anything—he was just going to screw up, and they just loved it.

James Welch

James Welch was born in 1940 in Browning, Montana. Black-feet on his father's side and Gros Ventre on his mother's, Welch attended schools on the Blackfeet and Fort Belknap reserva-tions in Montana as well as other places in the Northwest. He graduated from the University of Montana and then began a master's program in creative writing there. In addition he has worked as a laborer, forest-service employee, Indian firefighter, and counselor for Upward Bound at the University of Montana. Although a full-time writer, he occasionally teaches American Indian literature at the University of Washington and Cornell University.

He made his debut as a writer with the publication of his col-lected poems, Riding the Earthboy 40 *(1971). However, Welch is best known as a novelist. His* Winter in the Blood *(1974) received particularly high acclaim. The Death of Jim Loney (1979), his second novel, has also been widely praised. In both these works he offers a stunning, realistic portrait of the life on and off the Blackfeet Indian Reservation in Montana's empti-ness, the protagonists' sense of alienation, their detachment from old traditions, and their struggle to recover a distant past. An impressive use of humor, dry dialogue, and an attentive eye for detail are characteristics of Welch's narrative, together with a deliberately disjointed architecture reflecting his char-acters' psychological condition. His most recent work is a his-torical novel on the Blackfeet,* Fools Crow, *published in 1986 and named "Book of the Year" by the* Los Angeles Times.

Very much concerned with his responsibility as a writer dealing with Indian subjects, Welch firmly states that "for the most part only an Indian knows who he is—an individual who just happens to be an Indian—and if he has grown up on a reservation he will naturally write about what he knows. And hopefully he will have the toughness and fairness to present his material in a way that is not manufactured by conventional stance. . . . What I mean is—whites have to adopt a stance; Indians already have one."[1]

Welch and his wife, Lois, met me at the Missoula airport, and we went to an old train depot restaurant just outside the town. His calm, discreet, almost shy way of speaking blends with a sharp sense of humor, which comes out quietly, thus catching the listener totally off balance, just like his characters.

The interview took place the following day, September 12, 1985, at his home, not far from a gurgling stream, with a garden full of bushes and Montana wildflowers. A bleached, powerful deer skull rested on the grass nearby.

LC Would you speak about the storytelling tradition in your novels?

WELCH Well, I suppose first I should say that the novels are written in the Western, European-American tradition, which differs quite markedly from the storytelling tradition of the traditional Indians. For instance, in a novel you create a whole fictional world and you move characters through that, and in most novels I don't think an author has any sense of it really being instructional or having a moral at the end of it, which the stories usually did; they almost always did, they are instructional and had some kind of lesson to impart, especially to kids who were being formed, and the older people were trying to instill a sense of values in them. So, that's one difference I've noticed. As for a storyteller aspect, I just don't think of myself as a traditional storyteller, especially in the two novels *The Death of Jim Loney* and *Winter in the Blood*. I was trying to tell a story of certain people on or near reservations, the kind of problems they encounter. For instance, one is full-blooded Indian, and the other one is a half-breed Indian. So they have their own set of problems. So I don't know that I think in terms of telling the story; I think more in terms of characters and how you come to some sort of psychological crisis point or whatever. And therefore you have, after this point, some understanding of yourself, but you don't take responsibility for other people; you're just responsible only for yourself, to make yourself grow. So that's the kind of thing that I do in novels, and I can't really consider myself a traditional storyteller.

LC But what about the "crying for pity ritual" or "vision quest ritual" in *Winter in the Blood* and in *The Death of Jim Loney*?

WELCH Well, I don't know. Other people have told me these things exist, and in a sense I know kind of what people are getting at. Both characters are on a kind of search for something that will give some meaning to their lives. And I don't think either one of the people involved, the narrator or Jim Loney, knows particularly what he's looking for. But maybe the search itself will reveal something that will give meaning to his life.

LC Are you saying that the narrator or Jim Loney is not following a pattern?

WELCH No, I don't think so, I don't think it is a vision quest; it's hard for twentieth-century people actually to do a vision quest in that traditional way; in a sense, I guess, it has become a metaphysical vision quest or at least an abstract vision quest. I mean, in the real vision quest the people went to seek a vision and from that vision they would know how to conduct themselves, not only in their everyday lives, but in things that really counted for them, like in battle they'd been courageous. Depending upon which power animal appeared to them, they would take the attributes of that animal, so if a raven came to them, they would probably become farseeing, which in one sense would mean that they would probably be wise people. So, a traditional vision quest always had a particular thing that it sought and then once the vision came it had almost a practical aspect; then you could use the power that the vision represented. In a sense I can't see either character, in either novel, having finally received a vision; maybe the character in *Winter in the Blood*, when he tries to pull the cow out of the mud, when he learns who his grandfather is, has some small growth period; he seems to grow a little bit as a person, but not a lot, and those aren't the kind of visions upon which he can conduct his life from that point on. So, I'm not so sure that my supposed vision quest in those novels really came to the kind of fruition that a true vision quest comes to.

LC   Because of the approach to dreams and visions in Blackfeet culture, does you so-called surrealism come out from your tribal background? And can you call it "Blackfeet surrealism" then?

WELCH   I suppose in some sense. I mean, when you are immersed in the Indian culture, notions of reality just necessarily change because there is this tradition, which isn't far in the past. So I don't think it has had a chance to be extinguished entirely from the Blackfeet culture or any other northern plains cultures, which are the ones I know about. So, I think young people do have a notion of what their traditional forebears believed and how they saw life, how they saw their spiritual existence; and so, if you can see that and somehow translate it into contemporary experience I think you are being a part of that notion of reality, which to today's rational thinkers, I suppose, would be considered a form of surrealism.

LC   Owing to this Indian perspective, is the concept of time in your novels ritual and not a chronological one?

WELCH   I don't know, you're asking awfully good questions. In a sense I just do whatever seems to be right for me and never quite think in such terms, I guess. Oh, we're talking about time in terms of the course of the book? I just honestly don't know how to answer that. I think the time is chronological, certainly. I mean, they start at point A and they go to point Z, and several things happen to them in-between. I've had quite a bit of training as a poet. I wrote poetry for seven or eight years, and I learned from poetry a sense of economy of language, the sense of keeping the poem moving, keeping it jumping, don't dwell too much on transitions, that kind of thing; and so I think in a sense I've brought that kind of poetic technique to my writing, so even though it is chronological, it doesn't just happen by the numbers. I have a tendency to pick out scenes that I think would be important in the dramatic development of the story and of the characters, and I try not to dwell too much on moving from one place to another. So it's chronological, but yet I think it has a more poetic technique in the sense that I hope that my writing doesn't have too many wasted motions.

LC   Will you comment on Old Bird in *Winter in the Blood*; the
          Malcolm Lowry epigraph and its meaning in *The Death of Jim
          Loney*; indeed, "the horse in Blackfoot Indian culture" and in
          the fiction of James Welch?[2]

WELCH   Blackfeet, always Blackfeet. The old anthropologists say Black-
          foot. Well, the horse has always been important to Indian people,
          you know. When it came, it became really the primary way of
          moving around; it simplified their lives, made their lives a lot
          easier, also made their lives a little more adventuresome. A more
          economic way of killing buffalo, for instance, is to drive them
          over the cliff in a *pis'kun*, and a lot of them get slaughtered; you
          can butcher down there, and you have all the meat and hides
          you ever need. But as soon as the Blackfeet got the horse, they
          preferred to run the buffalo, and shoot him first with bow and
          arrows and later with rifles, because they liked the feeling that
          the horse had underneath them and the adventure of the chase
          itself. So the horse had a very number-one practical aspect; too,
          it had an aspect of sport; horse racing became very popular as
          well as this new method of hunting, which was almost a sport,
          and of course it had an almost religious part in their lives. For
          instance, the Blackfeet developed a horse culture in their later
          years; they felt that the horse deserves some place much like the
          buffalo did. Of course the buffalo was more natural because, as
          one book put it, it was their "stuff of life." From the buffalo they
          could get anything that they really needed in order to survive.
          The horse was certainly a tool of survival, but it was also some-
          thing that they felt had great significance in religious, ritualistic
          terms. So, when I write, the horse might have some significance,
          like Old Bird in *Winter in the Blood*. He had started out, I sup-
          pose, as just a cow horse, but later on he became something as a
          venerable old father, I guess. And also, the narrator felt that he
          too was in cahoots and was partially responsible for the death
          of his brother. So, that's why he thinks that Bird has carried
          the guilt all these years, and so together they tried to expiate
          the guilt in one scene in the novel. *Fools Crow*, you know, is
          set in the 1860s, so the horse is very much a part of their lives
          and again in a practical way, and as a way of measuring wealth.
          Nomadic tribes had to have portable wealth and what could be
          more portable than a horse or a herd of horses? So, in some ways

I'm still trying to figure out what the horse meant, because I'm talking from 1985, sitting in my living room, and the horses that I know now are all saddle horses, pleasure horses. Although I did take a ride up to the Blackfeet reservation and saw many herds of horses, and it occurred to me that I think Indians still measure, at least in some ways, their wealth in horses, just from seeing that number of herds of horses up on the reservation; the horse still means a great deal to the Blackfeet people.

LC Why the Malcolm Lowry epigraph?

WELCH The horse there represents a kind of freedom, I suppose, a sort of wistful desire to be free, "Ah, to have a horse and gallop away into the heart of all peace and simplicity in the world." You know the answer to that—the next word is no. So there's a sense of reality in this kind of flight of poetic fantasy; it's just that, you know; it's really no, it's the hard reality of that no which I felt applied to Jim Loney; sometimes he would have flights of fantasy and so on, but the hard reality is "no, you're caught in your situation for whatever reason," and I think he created his own situation and it wasn't going to be easy for him to get out of that.

LC A character in *Winter in the Blood* has raised many questions among the critics. Would you speak about the identity and role of the airplane man?

WELCH Well, I don't know, I don't think there is any terrific significance attached to him. You know, in one way I just wanted him as a kind of comic-relief character, who's blustery and full of himself and full of big ideas, I don't know, W. C. Fields-type character. In a sense he may be the most surrealistic character in the whole bunch, because—at least the way I tried to create him— you didn't know whether he had stolen this money or not, you didn't know if the cops were after him or not, and it's only when you see him being led out of that hotel room by the police that you realize that the guy was telling the truth all along. But I wanted him to be somebody to bang the narrator against, so that he would see this other world. And also he represents a kind of escape, the airplane man does. If the narrator goes with him to Canada and does this kind of thing, he might become something else, but the fact is they never get to make that trip, so he goes back home to the ranch. So the airplane man may have been something of an opportunity to the narrator that didn't come to pass.

LC   Does the title of your first novel, *Winter in the Blood*, convey the sense of the following stages in the narrator's tribal and personal life: winter 1883–84, the Blackfeet starved to death after the whites had killed off the buffalo; the narrator is frozen to spiritual death, "a servant to a memory of death." In the closing chapter is there a cleaning, purifying nature of winter?

WELCH   Well, winter certainly in that country is very treacherous. You're always aware of how vulnerable you are during the winter months. Most of the people live a fairly isolated life, and so if you don't do things properly, the winter could be treacherous and might even do you in. The thing about the narrator's father freezing to death in the wintertime is again based on something that does happen: Indians do get stuck in town for whatever reason, and they have to walk to wherever they live or to a cousin's house or whatever. And I'm sure if you've been near reservations you've seen Indians walking along the highway. So again that's based on a kind of sense of reality. I've known a couple of people who have frozen to death walking along the highway. So that isn't really much more than telling a kind of very real truth, that this does happen. The winter, I suppose, of *Winter in the Blood* has to do mostly with the character's feeling of distance —as he says, not only from; distance in terms of physical space, but distance in terms of mental space, emotional space, he feels as distance from his mother, distance from his grandmother, distance from the girl that he brought home. So the problem seems to lie within himself; and, I think, probably toward the end, by learning who his grandfather is, by saving the cow, by throwing his grandmother's tobacco pouch into her grave, maybe he has lessened that distance somewhat—that emotional distance —which probably would lead to a thawing of that winter in his blood.

LC   How could you define the very peculiar sense of humor you use in your novels?

WELCH   I think maybe a lot of it has to do with my own personality. When I sit by myself and write, I have a chance to elaborate on what might be humorous, not in a "belly-bustin' " way, but in a way that has a certain play on words or whatever, or I can create a character who's funny to me and I hope will be funny to other people, like Lame Bull. I think he's a funny character but other people might not find him funny. I noticed a lot of people have said they have found what they call "Indian humor" in that book, which is a humor based on presenting people in such a way that you're not exactly making fun of them, but you're seeing them for what they are and then you can tease them a little bit. That's a lot of Indian humor—teasing, and some plays on words; Indians are very good at puns. So I think some of it might have to do with that traditional Indian sense of humor that has survived for hundreds of years; teasing was always a great part of Indian humor, plus, I think, some of my own distorted sense of humor.

LC   Is Loney a sort of winner-as-loser in that he chooses the time and place of his own death?

WELCH   I think so. I think up to that point he hasn't done anything positive with his life, ever since high school ended. He was a basketball player; he was a smart young man, the kind of person the others got their answers from. He just sort of went into his drift: it happened; he went to the military. When he got out he'd take odd jobs, drink, and so on. He never developed himself and he knew that, I believe, but he was in a kind of spiral: he was finding himself more and more sitting in the kitchen, drinking wine. He was withdrawing from even his girlfriend, his sister, his partner, Pretty Weasel. When Pretty Weasel first sees him outside of the liquor store, he tries to sort of sneak away, but then they make up the plan to go hunting, Pretty Weasel does. And so his life is just one of drifting and also of an increasing reclusiveness. So, when he kills Pretty Weasel in the hunting trip, at that point he could have probably gone to the authorities and said, "This is what happened; it was an accident; I mistook him for a bear," or whatever, and he would have probably gotten off; they would have had no proof that he intended to shoot Pretty Weasel, but instead he chose to think of it himself: "possibly I pulled that trigger for some reason, maybe I did know it was Pretty Weasel." And so he chooses to run, to put himself on the run, and then, I think, he starts to formulate the plan to put into operation all these various clues and hints, so that finally he'll be standing on top of that cliff and Doore, the policeman—who he knows won't hesitate to shoot him—will be there with the rifle and will shoot him. So he does do this very well. He does orchestrate his own death very well, and I think he enjoys in a grim way doing that, so that he knows that finally it will come to this: him on the cliff, Doore taking the caps off his scope so he can line Loney up. So I think in some ways it's probably the only really positive thing that he does, and it's positive by being an act that he has created.

LC In the Bill Bevis interview you said that Elio Vittorini's *In Sicily* [1937] was a main influence for you in that he could use simple language poetically.[3] Would you elaborate on that?

WELCH Well, as I said, I'd been writing poetry exclusively for seven or eight years, and I was just totally immersed in the world of poetry. And so when it came time to think about writing a novel, I just had no idea how to do it; I didn't know much more than anybody else about plot or characters or whatever, and so I read a lot of books. I studied them and really tried to take them apart. How did that author develop that character, or how did he get these two people together. What kind of emotional relationship did they have? But most of the books were confusing. In some ways they were too intricate. So finally I found *In Sicily*, and I think it was a book written by a poet, which I was, so it was something I could really understand. It was a very simple story; they were things I could handle. In other words, I didn't need a whole sweep going on; I could work from scene to scene, just like Vittorini does. And I really loved the nature of the journey, that's what *In Sicily* is about, and how it begins. It begins almost on a whim; the protagonist gets the letter and he just goes to the train station and takes off. The interaction between him and his mother, between him and the knife grinder, between him and the Great Lombard, and the two suits on the train who were the Fascist police, I suppose. These were characters I could understand, and I knew what he was doing, and I knew the political aspects of the novel had to be such that he couldn't come right out and say who all these people represented and so on. There are just so many things about that novel that I liked, but mostly I really loved the writing. It's very poetically written. We were talking about surrealism earlier—it's just absolutely chock full of really believable, beautiful surrealism, and in some sense, I think, maybe I've tried to emulate his sense of surrealism.

LC   What about the non-Indian critics of your work and of American Indian literature in general?

WELCH For the most part I think they do a pretty good job. They're in some ways forced by their backgrounds and education and so on, to approach Indian literature from the outside, and of course they do study it quite a bit, so they do attempt to get a kind of comprehensive understanding of Indians as a whole, and then particular types of Indians. So I think, given those kinds of constrictions, I think they do a pretty good job, although they mostly end up talking about it in literary terms, or possibly even sociological terms. I don't think they can talk as confidently in cultural terms because they are not really quite as familiar with the culture as the people who are descendants and still partially immersed in that culture. I think, in all, they do a pretty good job. Although it's interesting they can take, like all critics, opposing views of the same book. You know, one will see it as a tragic novel, another will see it as a comic novel, and we don't know if that's possible. I don't know that there are enough Indian critics yet. Most Indian people so far seem to be the writers, and if there are critics among Indian people, it is the writers who perform that function. I think most Indian people who choose to go into some form of scholarship end up in history, or the social sciences, things like that; not many of them end up in literature.

LC   What about the European approach?

WELCH Well, I had a couple of experiences that are probably typical of the way some Europeans view American Indians. I was in Germany giving a reading and being on a panel at the American Studies Conference—I think it's an annual event. And Scott Momaday was there and a couple of other people were there, and we were on a panel. And most Germans had been raised on Indian stories written by this guy named Karl May. They were very romantic, you know, James Fenimore Cooper–type things, and the Indians were romantic heroic figures, while at the same time there were savages—the whole noble savage idea. But yet many of them— these were German professor-types—had been to America and most of them had been in the Southwest, and so they had really studied the Pueblo and Navajo cultures. That seems to be where Europeans end up in the Southwest, mainly, I think, because those cultures still have their traditions going; their language is still very strong, so I suppose they're the logical ones to study. But this one man rose up from the audience at one point and said: "Why didn't the Indians revolt against the government?" And he went on to point out that the blacks in the early sixties had trashed neighborhoods and so on and eventually got some sort of recognition, and maybe some of their problems were being corrected and so on. And so I think one of us tried to point out to him that the blacks usually lived in cities, in neighborhoods, in some of the larger, more powerful cities in the country, so when they revolted and started doing these acts of civil violence, they were paid attention to. And we pointed out that reservations are usually stuck out of the way, in unpopulated areas and it would be hard, say, if the Blackfeet people revolted on their reservation up in northwestern Montana. How would they coordinate with people in Oklahoma, Florida, or even the Dakotas, or whatever? So we tried to explain that, that it just won't have the same im- pact as the people revolting right there in the cities. And then we tried to point out that AIM had done a lot of good in that, because they did go to the cities, and they went to the places that had great symbolic importance to Americans, like Wounded Knee, and then of course to Mount Rushmore, Alcatraz Island, that kind of thing. So they actually went to those places and did get attention, and as a result they got some kind of reforms put through. So that's the way Europeans look at Indians; on one hand, they have a tendency to have the romantic view of the noble savage, and on the other hand they can't understand why present Indians don't improve their situations, because it seems like human nature to want to improve yourselves, and why do these people stay at the same level all the time? And so it's hard to explain that Indians do want to improve their situa- tion, but they can't. Part of it is just simply economic; there are no industries on most reservations, or if there is an industry it'll be a very small one, and it can't support a large number of people. So it's hard to get people to accept the reality, and it isn't just Europeans, incidentally: this is people from the East Coast, from California, or from the West Coast and other people in the suburban areas. They don't understand it. And they don't want to see the reality of the Indian situation.

LC   Can the study of literature be of any importance to the intercultural communications? How does it relate to this purpose?

WELCH   Well, I think it can be very simple if other cultures want to just take the time to read about another culture. I think most Indian writers would probably think that they are telling about a way of life, either traditional or contemporary, that Indians have led or are leading and this in essence is the truth of it. And so it's not a matter of Indian people, Indian writers, getting out whatever message they feel necessary; it's a question of people receiving that message. And unfortunately, the audience is quite small and it's quite ineffectual; a few university professors, a few people who are interested in Indians are out there, but it is not a very large audience yet, and I'm not sure it's going to get any larger, but it is also a very nonpowerful audience. The people who should be reading this and trying to understand more about Indians are people in the high government, people in industries that relate to Indian people. They are not reading this; they don't really care; the Indian problem is a problem that so far has been pretty well controlled, pretty well suppressed, and if they start paying too much attention to Indians, then they're going to have to do something about the Indian situation. So it's really advantageous for those kind of power people not to know anything about the culture.

LC   Do American Indian writers have a large audience among Indian people?

WELCH   I'm surprised—it's quite large, and it's partly due to certain people who are willing to teach it, I guess, on reservations or in universities. It's interesting, there are all these people who are willing to spread their position, their perception of Indian writing. And so, consequently, people like Leslie Silko, Momaday, Joy Harjo, Simon Ortiz—I could go on forever—they are actually being read all over the country, all over the United States, and of course even in other countries, in Europe. So I think there is a readership out there, a very loyal, sympathetic readership, but it's also a very small one. But among the Indian people, I am surprised when I go somewhere, to a reservation or to an urban Indian community, [and] they will have read my work and they will have read other people's work. So, yes, they do keep very well informed about literature; in fact it surprised me sometimes, that they do feel that they have the luxury, I guess, to sit and read a novel, for instance, or a book of poems or whatever. It's very encouraging.

LC   American Indian literature in mainstream American literature —what is its place and its contribution?

WELCH   First I have to kind of go back a little way, I think, to say D'Arcy McNickle probably started contemporary Indian literature, and at that point he was more noted as an anthropologist. So I think people thought, well, it's nice that D'Arcy was writing these books of fiction, but his real contribution is in the field of anthropology. So I don't think it was until 1969, when *House Made of Dawn* won the Pulitzer Prize and suddenly people started to notice Indian literature, that the way kind of opened for Indians; younger people too, younger people who didn't think that they had much of a chance as a writer, suddenly realized, well, an Indian can write. And so it cut both ways: young Indian people got a little confidence in themselves that maybe they could write too. And the mainstream of literature thought, gee, this book is pretty good and it won a prize. And so I think from that point on people have had to increasingly judge literature written by Indians on the standards that they judge literature written by anybody in this country. The level and the quality, it's all gone up, it's all been raised, from the beginning. In the beginning a lot of Indians didn't know how to write a poem; now they do. They are very sophisticated, and a young man like Ray Young Bear is just, you know, one of the best poets in America.

LC   Do you see any important change having taken place in your writing?

WELCH   Well, an important change has taken place with this last book. Usually I deal with an individual character and then I'll have some characters around that individual. But I've been more concerned with the things that an individual character encounters within the larger experience of a reservation or a small town, and then it might circle out to some place in northern Montana, so it might have reverberations like that. But now I'm working with the whole southern Blackfeet, the Pikuni people, and in this historical novel [*Fools Crow*], I'm telling it from their point of view, from the inside of their cultural point of view. And I'm sort of examining their lives, and also the lives of the encroaching people, the whites, but never from the white point of view; it's always from the Indian's. How they felt the pressure of this encroachment to them, and how it was driving them into a smaller and smaller area, and they were afraid they would be extinguished, they would be exterminated. Because there was a campaign in Montana in the 1860s to just exterminate these people, you know; they're in the way of manifest destiny, all that kind of stuff. So I'm dealing with a whole group of Indian people, and I'm dealing with their perception of this other cultural group that is coming in. It becomes obvious to them that this other group has much more power than they do. So, I guess I've gone from kind of the small look at one life and how it's affected by other people and situations to a culture, or at least a part of a culture, and how it's affected by a part of another culture.

LC   What writers are important to you?

WELCH   Well, let's see. They are the traditional ones, I suppose. Hemingway, certainly, because he had such a very vivid economical style that I think a poet could relate to; a lot of other American writers probably around this time. John Steinbeck I've felt very strongly influenced by. And a lot of the influence has just kind of sunk in without my having known it. Some of my contemporaries, I always read their books, and I'm sure some of their influence will sink in on me. And then of course when you read people like Momaday or Silko, and some of the other people who write fiction, other Indian people, I think they influence me quite a bit. And of course the books that I have studied about the Blackfeet people have had some influence, importance. I really can't say that it's been particular writers who have had a great influence on me, or whose work I consider important above other kinds of work: I just read practically anything, and I think I can gain something out of practically anything.

LC   Could you describe your writing process?

WELCH   It kind of evolved into a pattern, I think. I usually think quite a bit about the novel before I even start it; while I'm mowing the lawn, or fishing or whatever, I'll be thinking about maybe some characters, or certain aspects of plot or where I want this piece of writing to end up. And I'll just carry it around in my head, sort of elaborating for several months, and then after a while I might start making some notes and draw some characters. I'll even have sort of a minimal outline which just is the beginning and ending and maybe three or four high point of this novel I'd like to write. And at that point I've pretty much got everything I need, and so I just sit down and start writing. And I try to work four or five hours a day, pretty consistently, because once you leave something like that, it's really hard to get back, so you've got to go, if you're on a roll you've got to keep going. So that's pretty much how I write. And I go all the way through a first draft, and then I go back and start on another draft. So it's mostly just kind of the stages of thinking about it, and then making some notes, and then actually sitting down and writing.

LC   You talked before of your new novel. Do you have any other work in progress?

WELCH   I have maybe two or three ideas for things to do, none of which include another novel right now, but poetry, and maybe a series of small vignettes that I've been kind of working on. But I wanted it to be kind of a little mini-emblematic novel. I mean, I want them all to be related—beginning and ending. So I expect eventually another idea for a novel will sneak into my mind. I have certainly got enough ideas for them, but no particular one stronger than the other yet.

Notes

INTRODUCTION

1 Walter Mauro. "L'intervista letteraria: Lo scrittore e il potere." Paper read at the conference "L'intervista strumento di documentazione: Giornalismo, Antropologia, Storia Orale," Rome, May 5–7, 1986.
2 Interviews with Gerald Vizenor and Simon Ortiz (all interviews cited are from this volume); N. Scott Momaday, "The Man Made of Words," in *The First Convocation of American Indian Scholars*, ed. Rupert Costo (San Francisco: Indian Historian Press, 1970), p.49.
3 Interviews with N. Scott Momaday and Ortiz.
4 Interview with Momaday.
5 Interview with Wendy Rose.
6 Ibid.
7 Interview with Momaday.
8 Interview with Linda Hogan.
9 Interview with Ortiz.
10 Interview with Hogan.
11 Kenneth Lincoln, *Native American Renaissance* (Berkeley and Los Angeles: University of California Press, 1983), p.1.

PAULA GUNN ALLEN

1 Paula Gunn Allen, review of *This Bridge Called My Back: Writings by Radical Women of Color*, ed. Cherrie Moraga and Gloria Anzaldua, *Conditions Eight* 3 (Spring 1982): 127.

MICHAEL DORRIS AND LOUISE ERDRICH

1 *Medicina d'amore* (Milan: Mondadori, 1985).

Notes

JOY HARJO

1 In Joseph Bruchac, ed., *Songs from This Earth on Turtle's Back* (Greenfield, NY: Greenfield Review Press, 1983), p.92.
2 Joy Harjo, "New Orleans" and "Skeleton of Winter," in *She Had Some Horses* (New York: Thunder's Mouth Press, 1983), pp.42, 31.
3 In Bruchac, *Songs from This Earth*, p.92.
4 Audre Lorde, "The Transformation of Silence into Language and Action," in *Sister Outsider: Essays and Speeches* (Trumansburg, NY: Crossing Press, 1984), p.41.
5 In Joseph Bruchac, "Interview with Joy Harjo," *North Dakota Quarterly* 53 (Spring 1985), p.227.
6 In Bruchac, *Songs from This Earth*, p.92.

LINDA HOGAN

1 Linda Hogan, "Autobiographical Sketch," *Sun Tracks* 5 (1979): 78.
2 Linda Hogan, "The Transformation of Tribalism," *Book Forum* 5, no.3 (1980): 403–409.
3 Linda Hogan, "Native American Women: Our Voice, the Air," *Frontiers* 6, no.3 (Fall 1981): 1–4. Special Issue on Native American Women, edited by Linda Hogan.
4 Audre Lorde, *Sister Outsider: Essays and Speeches* (Trumansburg, NY: Crossing Press, 1984).

N. SCOTT MOMADAY

1 N. Scott Momaday, *The Way to Rainy Mountain* (Albuquerque: University of New Mexico Press, 1969), p.4.
2 N. Scott Momaday, "A First American Views His Land," *National Geographic Magazine* 150, no.1 (1976): 18; Momaday, "A Special Sense of Place," *Viva* (May 7, 1972): 2, italics mine.
3 N. Scott Momaday, "Carriers of the Dream Wheel," in *Angle of Geese and Other Poems* (Boston: David R. Godine, 1974), p.42.
4 N. Scott Momaday, "Learning from the Indian," *Viva* (July 9, 1972): 2.
5 N. Scott Momaday, "The Morality of Indian Hating," *Ramparts* 3, no.1 (Summer 1964): 36.

SIMON ORTIZ

1 In Bo Schöler, ed., *Coyote Was Here* (Aarhus, Denmark: Seklos, 1984), p.65.

2 Simon Ortiz, "Songs, Poetry, and Language: Expression and Perception" (Tsaile, Ariz.: Navajo Community College Press, 1977).

3 N. Scott Momaday, "The Man Made of Words," in *The First Convocation of American Indian Scholars*, ed. Rupert Costo (San Francisco: Indian Historian Press, 1970), pp.49–84.

4 Geary Hobson, "Remembering the Earth," in *The Remembered Earth*, ed. Geary Hobson (Albuquerque: Red Earth Press, 1979), p.11.

5 Geary Hobson, "The Rise of the White Shaman as a New Version of Cultural Imperialism," and Leslie Silko, "An Old-Time Attack Conducted in Two Parts," in Hobson, *The Remembered Earth*, pp.100–108, 211–16. Wendy Rose, "Just What's All This Fuss about Whiteshamanism Anyway," in Schöler, *Coyote Was Here*, pp.13–24.

WENDY ROSE

1 In Joseph Bruchac, ed., *Songs from This Earth on Turtle's Back* (Greenfield, NY: Greenfield Review Press, 1983), p.207.

2 In Dexter Fisher, ed., *The Third Woman* (Boston: Houghton Mifflin, 1980), p.85.

3 Wendy Rose, *Builder Kachina: A Home-Going Cycle* (Marvin, SD: Blue Cloud Quarterly Press, 1979), p.14.

4 In Joseph Bruchac, "The Bones Are Alive," in *Survival This Way: Interviews with American Indian Poets*, ed. Joseph Bruchac, Sun Tracks Series 15 (Tucson: University of Arizona Press, 1987).

5 The interview with Carol Hunter appeared in Schöler, *Coyote Was Here*, pp.40–56.

6 Ibid., p.45.

7 Geary Hobson, "The Rise of the White Shaman as a New Version of Cultural Imperialism," in Hobson, *The Remembered Earth*, pp.100–108.

LESLIE MARMON SILKO

1 Leslie Marmon Silko, *Storyteller* (New York: Seaver Books, 1981), p.6.

2 In Per Seyersted, "Two Interviews with Leslie Marmon Silko," *American Studies in Scandinavia* 13, no.1 (1981): 24.

GERALD VIZENOR

1 Gerald Vizenor, *Wordarrows: Indians and Whites in the New Fur Trade* (Minneapolis: University of Minnesota Press, 1978), pp.vii, viii.

2 Gerald Vizenor, "Indians at the Guthrie," in *Voices of the Rainbow*, ed. Kenneth Rosen (New York: Viking, 1975), p.31; Vizenor, *Earthdivers: Tribal Narratives of Mixed Descent* (Minneapolis: University of Minnesota Press, 1978), p.ix.

3 Vizenor, *Wordarrows*, p.17.

4 Gerald Vizenor, *The People Named the Chippewa: Historical Narratives* (Minneapolis: University of Minnesota Press, 1984), p.130.

5 Gerald Vizenor, *Darkness in Saint Louis Bearheart* (Minneapolis: Truck Press, 1978), p.185.

6 Gerald Vizenor, "Socioacupuncture: Mythic Reversals and Striptease in Four Scenes," in *The American Indian and the Problems of History*, ed. Calvin Martin (New York: Oxford University Press, 1987), 180–91.

7 Gerald Vizenor, "Chair of Tears," in *Earthdivers*, p.24.

JAMES WELCH

1 In John R. Milton, ed., *American Indian II* (Vermillion: University of South Dakota Press, 1971), p.54.

2 John C. Ewers, *The House in Blackfoot Indian Culture* (Washington: Smithsonian Institution Press, 1955).

3 In Bill Bevis, "Dialogue with James Welch," *Northwest Review* 20, nos.2–3 (1982): 163–85.

Selected Bibliography

PAULA GUNN ALLEN

The Blind Lion. Berkeley: Thorp Spring Press, 1974. Poetry.

A Cannon between My Knees. New York: Strawberry Press, 1981. Poetry.

Coyote's Daylight Trip. Albuquerque: La Confluencia, 1978. Poetry.

The Sacred Hoop: Recovering the Feminine in American Indian Tradition. Boston: Beacon Press, 1986. Nonfiction.

Shadow Country. Los Angeles: UCLA American Studies Center Press, 1982. Poetry.

Skins and Bones. Albuquerque: West End Press, 1988. Poetry.

Spider Woman's Granddaughters: Traditional Tales and Contemporary Writing by Native American Women. Edited by Paula Gunn Allen. Boston: Beacon Press, 1989. Oral literature and short fiction.

Star Child. Marvin, SD: Blue Cloud Quarterly Press, 1981. Poetry.

Studies in American Indian Literature: Critical Essays and Course Designs. Edited by Paula Gunn Allen. New York: Modern Language Association, 1983. Nonfiction.

The Woman Who Owned the Shadows. San Francisco: Spinsters Ink, 1983. Fiction.

Wyrds. San Francisco: Taurean Horn Press, 1987. Poetry.

MICHAEL DORRIS

The Broken Cord: One Family's Ongoing Struggle with Fetal Alcohol Syndrome. New York: Harper and Row, 1989. Nonfiction.

With Arlene Hirschfelder and Mary Lou Byler. *A Guide to Research on North American Indians.* Chicago: American Library Association, 1983. Nonfiction.

Native Americans: Five Hundred Years After. Photographs by Joseph
    Farber. New York: Thomas Y. Crowell, 1977. Nonfiction.
A Yellow Raft in Blue Water. New York: Henry Holt, 1987. Fiction.

LOUISE ERDRICH

Baptism of Desire: Poems. New York: Harper and Row, 1989. Poetry.
The Beet Queen. New York: Henry Holt, 1986. Fiction.
Imagination. Columbus, Ohio: Charles Merrill, 1981. Children's litera-
    ture.
Jacklight. New York: Holt, Rinehart and Winston, 1984. Poetry.
Love Medicine. New York: Holt, Rinehart and Winston, 1984. Fiction.
Tracks. New York: Henry Holt, 1988. Fiction.

JOY HARJO

In Mad Love and War. Middletown, Conn.: Wesleyan University Press,
    1990. Poetry.
The Last Song. Las Cruces, NM: Puerto del Sol Press, 1975. Poetry.
Secrets from the Center of the World. Photographs by Steve Strom.
    Sun Tracks Series. Tucson: University of Arizona Press, 1989. Non-
    fiction.
She Had Some Horses. New York: Thunder's Mouth Press, 1983. Poetry.
What Moon Drove Me to This. New York: I. Reed Books, 1979. Poetry.

LINDA HOGAN

Calling Myself Home. Greenfield Center, NY: Greenfield Review Press,
    1979. Poetry.
Daughters, I Love You. Denver, Colo.: Loretto Heights College, 1981.
    Poetry.
Eclipse. Los Angeles: UCLA American Indian Studies Center Press,
    1983. Poetry.
Mean Spirit. New York: Random House. Forthcoming. Fiction.
Seeing through the Sun. Amherst: University of Massachusetts Press,
    1985. Poetry.
With Judith McDaniel and Carol Bruchac, eds. *The Stories We Hold
    Secret*. Greenfield Center, NY: Greenfield Review Press, 1986. Non-
    fiction.
With Charles Colbert Henderson (Hogan's father). *That Horse*. Acoma,
    NM: Acoma Press, 1985. Short fiction.

N. SCOTT MOMADAY

The Ancient Child. New York: Doubleday, 1989. Fiction.

Angle of Geese and Other Poems. Boston: David R. Godine, 1974. Poetry.

Colorado: Summer, Fall, Winter, Spring. Text by N. Scott Momaday. Photography by David Muench. New York: Rand McNally, 1973. Nonfiction.

The Complete Poems of Frederick Goddard Tuckerman. Edited by N. Scott Momaday. New York: Oxford University Press, 1965. Poetry.

The Gourd Dancer. New York: Harper and Row, 1976. Poetry.

House Made of Dawn. New York: Harper and Row, 1968. Fiction.

The Journey of Tai-Me. Santa Barbara, Calif.: Privately printed, 1967. Nonfiction.

The Names: A Memoir. New York: Harper and Row, 1976. Nonfiction.

The Way to Rainy Mountain. Albuquerque: University of New Mexico Press, 1969. Nonfiction.

SIMON ORTIZ

Blue and Red. Acoma, NM: Acoma Partners in Basics, 1982. Children's literature.

With Rudolfo A. Anaya, eds. *Ceremony of Brotherhood.* Albuquerque: Academia Publications, 1981. Nonfiction.

Earth Power Coming: Short Fiction in Native American Literature. Edited by Simon Ortiz. Tsaile, Ariz.: Navajo Community College Press, 1983. Short fiction.

Fight Back: For the Sake of the People, for the Sake of the Land. Institute for Native American Development Literary Journal 1, no.1, Native American Studies. Albuquerque: University of New Mexico, 1980. Poetry.

Fightin': New and Collected Stories. New York: Thunder's Mouth Press, 1983. Short fiction.

From Sand Creek. New York: Thunder's Mouth Press, 1981. Poetry.

Going for the Rain. New York: Harper and Row, 1976. Poetry.

A Good Journey. Berkeley: Turtle Island Press, 1977. Poetry.

Howbah Indians. Tucson: Blue Moon Press, 1978. Fiction.

The Importance of Childhood. Acoma, NM: Acoma Partners in Basics, 1982. Children's literature.

Naked in the Wind. Pembroke, NC: Quetzal-Vihio Press, 1971. Poetry.

With Sharol Graves. *The People Shall Continue.* San Francisco: Children's Book Press, 1978. Children's literature.

A Poem Is a Journey. Bourbonnais, Ill.: Ptranadon Press, 1981. Poetry.

Selected Bibliography

WENDY ROSE

Academic Squaw. Marvin, SD: Blue Cloud Quarterly Press, 1977. Poetry.

Builder Kachina: A Home-Going Cycle. Marvin, SD: Blue Cloud Quarterly Press, 1979. Poetry.

The Halfbreed Chronicles and Other Poems. Los Angeles: West End Press, 1985. Poetry.

Hopi Roadrunner Dancing. Greenfield Center, NY: Greenfield Review Press, 1973. Poetry.

Long Division: A Tribal History. New York: Strawberry Press, 1976. Poetry.

Lost Copper. Banning, Calif.: Malki Museum Press, 1980. Poetry.

What Happened When the Hopi Hit New York. New York: Contact II, 1982. Poetry.

LESLIE MARMON SILKO

The Almanac of the Dead. New York: Simon and Schuster. Forthcoming. Fiction.

Ceremony. New York: Viking Press, 1977. Fiction.

The Delicacy and Strength of Lace: Letters between Leslie Marmon Silko and James Wright, edited by Anne Wright. Saint Paul, Minn.: Graywolf Press, 1986. Nonfiction.

Laguna Woman. Greenfield Center, NY: Greenfield Review Press, 1974. Poetry.

Storyteller. 1981. New York: Arcade, 1989. Short fiction, poems, and autobiography.

GERALD VIZENOR

Darkness in Saint Louis Bearheart. Minneapolis: Truck Press, 1978. Fiction.

Earthdivers: Tribal Narratives of Mixed Descent. Minneapolis: University of Minnesota Press, 1978. Short fiction and essays.

Empty Swings. Minneapolis: Nodin Press, 1967. Haiku.

Escorts to White Earth: One Hundred Years on a Reservation. Minneapolis: Four Winds, 1968. Nonfiction.

The Everlasting Sky: New Voices from the People Named the Chippewa. New York: Macmillan, 1972. Nonfiction.

Griever: An American Monkey King in China. New York: Fiction Collective; Normal: Illinois State University, 1987. Fiction.

Harold of Orange. 1983. Film and unpublished Screenplay.

Matsushima: Pine Island. Minneapolis: Nodin Press, 1984. Haiku.

The People Named the Chippewa: Historical Narratives. Minneapolis: University of Minnesota Press, 1984. Nonfiction.

Raising the Moon Vines. Minneapolis: Nodin Press, 1964. Haiku.

Seventeen Chirps. Minneapolis: Nodin Press, 1965. Haiku.

With Jerome Downes. *Slights Abrasions: A Dialogue in Haiku*. Minneapolis: Nodin Press, 1966. Haiku.

Summer in the Spring: Ojibwe Lyric Poems and Tribal Stories. Minneapolis: Nodin Press, 1981. Originally published 1970 under the titles *anishinabe nagamon* and *anishinabe adisokan*. Nonfiction.

Tribal Scenes and Ceremonies. Minneapolis: Nodin Press, 1976. Nonfiction.

The Trickster of Liberty. Minneapolis: University of Minnesota Press, 1988. Fiction.

Two Wings the Butterfly. Minneapolis: Privately printed, 1962. Haiku.

Wordarrows: Indians and Whites in the New Fur Trade. Minneapolis: University of Minnesota Press, 1978. Short fiction and essays.

JAMES WELCH

The Death of Jim Loney. New York: Harper and Row, 1979. Fiction.

Fools Crow. New York: Viking Press, 1986. Fiction.

With Ripley S. Hugo and Lois M. Welch, eds. *The Real West Marginal Way: A Poet Autobiography*. New York: Norton, 1986. Nonfiction.

Riding the Earthboy 40. New York: World Publishing, 1971. Poetry.

Winter in the Blood. New York: Harper and Row, 1974. Fiction.

Photo Credits